Low Hanging Fruit
And Highly Placed Vegetables
Ripe or Rotten Leadership

Tom Fehlman
Edited Rhonda Frith-Lyons

authorHOUSE®

AuthorHouse™
1663 Liberty Drive
Bloomington, IN 47403
www.authorhouse.com
Phone: 1-800-839-8640

First published by AuthorHouse   11/1/2011

ISBN: 978-1-4634-4815-8 (sc)
ISBN: 978-1-4634-4814-1 (hc)
ISBN: 978-1-4634-4813-4 (e)

Library of Congress Control Number: 2011914254

Printed in the United States of America

Dedication

I'm going to avoid the usual platitudes of dedicating this book to specific friends, family and significant others. I received help and encouragement from many. Mike Harding, my friend and business manager for over twenty five years is first and foremost. However, if forced to choose one person who kicked me into gear, my granddaughter Peyton comes immediately to mind. However, every day for the past thirty years I've gotten new "material" from well-intended but ill-prepared managers who "fill up cemeteries" while completing their tasks. So I must at least recognize their contributions. Without them, I would not need to write this book. Nor would I be able to make a living as a Leadership Consultant. Good managers must be good Leaders. Good Leaders can get others to manage for them. Today far too many managers are pretending to be leaders. Good Leaders don't walk past emotional and behavioral "fruit" their people give them every day.

I will also point out that there are multitudes of people getting "dumped on" daily by managers who have been given some misguided notion that they are leaders. Our people keep giving us obvious signals and clues as to where they are and what they're feeling. As Leaders, if we keep in balance between task and relationship, we will hear them and feel their pain. But many managers and executives remain above the fray. They walk past people every day doing good work without acknowledgement of their efforts, because they're too busy looking for problems. "Urgent" defines the next pile of work on the desk, but that pile allows many of us to say we don't have time to coach and encourage our people. It's time to start "reading the tea leaves" and following the signs. So, for the multitudes of good folks out there doing a good job that goes unnoticed, or maybe needing a little help and coaching that you don't get, you have my understanding, sympathy and support. This book is also written with you in mind. Hopefully somehow, in some way, if this book helps managers to become leaders, your pain will ease.

> **Δ Low hanging fruit has usually been put there by highly-placed vegetables.**
>
> Tom Fehlman

Contents

Forward Is Forearmed

The content of this book has been accumulating over the past thirty years. So, why am I writing this book now? There are at least three salient reasons that come to mind.

First, hopefully this book will get all those people who have been bugging me to write a book for the past thirty years off my back. Second, experts in the field tell me it's good therapy to talk through all the management "scar tissue" I've accumulated over the past thirty years.

Leadership Consulting can be a painful experience, if you're doing it for the right reasons. It is time to Vent!! Third; I'm getting too old to keep busting my butt teaching leadership skills to managers and their respective organizations that aren't committed to change, or applying common sense. Good leadership is not "rocket science". It is about thinking as a Behaviorist.

And since Behavior Management cannot be dealt with in absolute terms, Leadership is primarily about the consideration of options and risks. Authors who use theorems and equations to exhibit their expertise on the subject of leadership probably haven't "been there and done that".

In my humble (okay, so maybe not so humble) opinion, If you haven't loaded trucks to make a living, or worked on a swing shift in a manufacturing plant or similar experiences, you shouldn't be telling others what leadership is about. If you haven't managed in both a union and union-free environment, you're in no position to tell either side how to lead.

When you've seen the pain of young Engineers struggling with their new and uncomfortable roles of Managers, you may be in a position to guide others through their leadership survival training. You can't learn leadership in an ivory tower. Leadership is simply good balance between task and relationship, and avoiding extremes whenever possible.

However, for some reason the "urgency of the task" continues to warp and thwart organizational development and the redefinition of workplace relationships that are demanding change. We continue to act "Tactical", when we need to be thinking Strategically.

Years ago Robert Blake and Jane Mouton captured this balance in their "[1]Managerial Grid". The optimum level where a leader can perform contains both a high concern for production and a high concern for people. Situational Leadership will cause fluctuations in the balance from time to time, but ultimately good Leaders make decisions in balance between the two drivers of task and relationship.

When I think of balance, two long-term clients and long-time friends come to mind. Mark Pringle is a high level operations manager and Mike Shaum is a HR Manager. They have been together at several locations over a period of time, and they remind me of "a little bit country, and a little bit rock n' roll".

Years ago over lunch they figured out they actually had common causes. Mark was and is obviously more balanced on the task side. Mike is more balanced from the Human Resources side. A manufacturing plant within their company historically and repetitively had labor issues, and had gone through a series of managers and HR Managers. Several years ago Mark was asked to go to this location and create both stability and productivity, which was not going to be an easy task based on the plant history.

He asked Mike to relocate with him, and take over the Human Resource function, which was in total chaos. Obviously they were successful or I wouldn't mention them. Productivity is up and chaos is down. Mark gives people a sense of security with his operational leadership, and Mike lets them know the company cares about them with his walk around leadership, sense of humor and openness to stop, talk and listen. Balance between task and relationship can occur collectively as well as individually.

---

1   Robert Blake, Jane Mouton *Managerial Grid* (Gulf Publishing, 1994)

I want to thank all the outstanding managers and leaders who have contributed and continue adding to this book. I have taught and assessed tens of thousands of managers and supervisors, and I continue to learn much more from them than they can possibly learn from me. This book is also dedicated to all the subordinates who have to wade through the chaos and obstacles that poor and ineffective management daily heaps upon them.

Incidentally, if you are presently a manager, how many of your people wake up in the morning and say "Wow, I can't wait to get to work today!" That's an important question we don't ask ourselves enough. Through informal surveys over the past twenty-five years my belief is that most people view their work as a place and not an activity.

They have limited input into the direction and results of their personal drivers, so they engage, but are not engaged. It is not by accident that most morale surveys done in the past twenty years demonstrate that most employees feel that the most important attribute their leaders can possess is caring enough to listen to them. It's ironic that possibly the most important skill managers can apply is the leadership skill of active listening. It doesn't cost anything to get, and it doesn't cost anything to use.

Personally, I couldn't continue to handle the hypocrisy of ill-prepared people playing the "game" of leadership at my expense, so I started my own company twenty two years ago at their expense. I don't believe I will ever run out of clients that are "over managed" and "under led". Now I can choose who to work with, based on how trainable and change oriented I think they are. Lack of skill doesn't bother me nearly as much as the lack of initiative. I can give leadership skills to those who want to learn. There is not much I can do, or am moved to do, with those who believe there is no room for improvement.

My company is one of the few consulting firms around that has the nerve to actually guarantee outcomes or there is no charge for the service. The day my company can't ethically bill for our work is the day I retire. If Leadership is an ethical endeavor, so then must be the training of Leadership.

Many people (including clients) tell me I would now be impossible to manage because of my "clarity" in stating my positions, so I better stick to this consulting gig. I am very proud to wear the moniker of "Non

Manageable", as long as my family understands that I somewhat feebly attempt to remain totally manageable in my personal life.

This book is also especially dedicated to my beautiful and wise twelve year old granddaughter, Peyton, who continues to remind me that another day brings more opportunities to "get it right".

It bothers me greatly to know that one day she may grow up to be managed by the type of so-called leader this book takes to task. However, already in her short tenure she has demonstrated that she will not tolerate inattention and poor management very long. I hope she does not turn into one of those "deteriorated children" we call adults too quickly.

Δ **If you don't do everything you can to change it; you lose the right to bitch about it.**

Tom Fehlman

Chapter 1: Seeds of Leadership

Leadership Defines Who You Are; Not What You Do!!

I have assessed over 7000 participants for all types of leadership positions, and I have taught thousands of participants in leadership skills and practices, including combined sessions of supervisors and shop stewards. I am absolutely and firmly convinced that becoming a leader is "A Calling", rather than the next "rung on the ladder". Good leaders are passionate about what they do and who they do it with. If you are engaged in an interview for some type of leadership position, and the question is asked "Why do you want to be a leader?" what will the answer be?

Is it simply the next step in a pre-determined career path? Is there pressure from home to make more money? Is there a high need for power and control? Do you do things to make other people successful, or do you do it for selfish reasons? I follow up this question with another one: "What have you done to prepare yourself for a leadership position?

More often than not the reaction to this question is dead silence. If you were hiring for a leadership position, without factoring in past task achievements, would you hire someone who has done nothing to prepare for the position? Yet we hire these folks every day for the wrong reasons, only to come back later with wonderment and surprise that they didn't turn out so well.

My dad was a master toolgrinder for the Bendix Corporation, who at the time made air brakes for many and various industries. He loved what he did, and he was a master at it. Many times management came to him and asked him to take a supervisor job. Every time he turned them down. He had found his calling. He loved to work with his hands. He was challenged in grinding tools down to impossible dimensions. The only power and control he needed was that job sitting squarely in front of him.

Passion brings about pride, and he had plenty of both when he talked about his job. From my point of view he didn't make enough money. There were many times we struggled through union strikes and layoffs, which would not have affected him and my family if he had chosen to become part of management. Although he had to belong to a union, he certainly did not love the union, and most certainly did not overall benefit from his membership with the union.

When he went on strikes, he had to take menial and often very physical jobs that would have challenged many people much younger than he, simply to keep food on the table. One of the reasons I engage in union avoidance work from time to time is because of what the union did to my dad and my family. But I never heard him complain; because these were simply trials and tribulations he and we had to go through in order for him to get back to what he loved to do- grind tools down to impossible tolerances.

Looking back on those days, so many years later, I deeply regret that I was not much more supportive of who he was, and what he loved. Like many of you, I had to work through high school and college to make enough money to go to college, because there was no money from my parents to help me along. I resented the fact that I had to load trucks during the week and weekends, rather than going to ballgames and parties with my friends.

I never asked for money, because I knew there wasn't any, and there were times I resented the hell out of my situation. Now I wish I could go back and tell him how much I respect his calling and his passion. His work defined his personal value system. It is somewhat ironic that we often pass on to our children and employees both good and bad attributes by accident, and not by design.

It's certainly possible and maybe even probable that you do not feel driven to be a leader. In my simplistic world there are many reasons you shouldn't be a leader, and only a few why you should. But those few reasons why you should are non-negotiable. My sentries are always on alert for people who want to become leaders for the wrong reasons. I look for, enjoy and admire all the true professionals in all walks of life I encounter every day. I encounter floor sweepers who have elevated floor sweeping into an art form.

I encounter bar tenders who love what they do, and at times I may even get "over-served" by them. I run into machine operators who leave their machines when I enter their workspace, and politely remind me they require ear protection in their work areas. I work with sales people who love the "thrill of the chase" as they describe it. Leadership in its purest form is truly a calling. It defines who you are or are striving to be and, who and what you care for.

True professionals and "Masters" of any profession are first measured "Around Their Heart". You should never see descriptors such as "drive, commitment, loyalty, or enthusiasm" in a written job description. I can be committed for instance, but not show observable enthusiasm. So which one is more important? Behaviors are hard to qualify and consistently measure. If you don't get up every morning excited about the possibilities and challenges that a new day brings, you are in the wrong job. I can't measure it, but I will know if you got it. That's a free lesson you can thank my old man for.

Δ Leaders are Measured Around Their Hearts

Tom Fehlman

And a Young Child Shall Lead Them

Recently I received the highest form of recognition that in my world is possible to obtain. I wasn't consciously trying to get it, and I'm not sure I'm worthy of it. My granddaughter Peyton, with whom I have had almost daily contact since she was born, achieved a significant milestone in her young life of twelve years.

She was selected by her teachers to attend the National Young Leaders Conference (NYLC) being held in Washington, D.C. For a full week she attended conferences with Congressional leaders, visited famous landmarks, and participated daily in leadership workshops with other kids from around the country. For the first time in her life she was in the total control of folks other than family members. Parents and grandparents were not allowed even visitation rights during the week. Interesting that no contact seemed to concern the rest of us a great deal more than it concerned her.

I thought… "That's not about to happen". So I made arrangements to take her to D.C., and let her know I would be in the general area if she needed us in an emergency. I would be out of sight and probably out of mind, but at least I could get to her quickly if she needed me. Unbeknownst to me, she had to submit an essay on leadership to the conference before she attended. She had to do this without any help, ideas or suggestions from others. Peyton's mother thought I would find the final product interesting reading. I pass it on in hopes you will also. The sentence structure is not perfect, but not bad for a twelve year old. You'll get the idea. The essay is as follows:

What It Takes to be a Leader

Leader, the dictionary says that this word means a person or thing that leads, as simple as that, but this does not include what it takes to lead. It's not just leading that makes you a leader it is your skills and even your attributes. It is how you react to situations and how you make decisions.

Well, my role model is someone who knows leadership very well and is and has to be a leader everyday because his job is to teach leadership and management skills to business owners and managers. He is my grandfather. But his job is not what makes him a leader to me, it is personality, the way when he makes a promise he never breaks it, his kindness, his jokes, and even his sternness. He makes decisions that may not be the best for the present but will come out perfect in the long run.

For example this summer we had planned on going to Canada to visit his family but he gave that up so I could have the once in a lifetime experience to come here, to JrNYLC. Of course we all know that a good leader can't always be nice. He is not shy to tell when I'm doing something wrong or something that I shouldn't be.

*So based on my grandfather **my** definition of a leader is…*

Leader: A loving person with good decision making skills, a person who knows right from wrong and is not afraid to tell you what you are doing wrong and how to do it right. A person with care and honesty. A person like my grandfather.

I hope and pray that she never finds out that I'm not that good. She'll probably figure it out when she reads this book. The first thing that struck me when I read Peyton's essay was "Wow, I'm pretty damn good". The second thing I thought about is that I hoped she was talking about me and not her other grandfather. The next thought to hit me was how proud I was of my precious granddaughter.

The reason why her essay is in this book is that, upon reflection this child of twelve years has captured in such beautiful and concise terms what a leader is and what a leader does. She doesn't have her MBA (but she just received her grade school diploma). She has yet to attend one of my workshops since I occasionally use "colorful" language and exhibit irrational passion about the points I'm trying to make.

She has never read a Covey or Drucker book about leadership. Possibly I've unintentionally given to her what my dad gave to me. Frankly, it appears to me we may all end up reading a book on leadership she writes some day.

Bosses need submissive people who will obey without question. Managers need titles for recognition and validation. True leaders don't have to try to get peoples' attention through artificial means or management "techniques". They just have it. More importantly, they serve as examples and models for those who would follow them in leadership roles.

Why Now? Why Not

There is nothing new here. If this was rocket science, I sure wouldn't be writing about it. That's really the point. Everybody is looking for the panacea, the gimmick, the "cure all" of all the leadership woes that abound. Some training organizations and management authors have figured out that if they can find a unique twist, like renaming a rock as a "hard substance", they can actually fool people into thinking they've discovered something new.

More importantly, so-called decision makers are willing to spend a lot of money for this new "hard substance" when they already have a bunch of rocks sitting in storage they've never used. Go in the storage room and look at your rock collections gathering dust. Juran, Deming, Quality Circles, TPM (Total Process Management) SPC (Statistical Process Control) and countless other iterations are becoming distant memories. Six Sigma and Synchronous Flow are the new buzzwords.

Behavior Modification has become Interactive Management. Participative Management techniques have become 7 Habits. And so on and so on. The truth is, we don't stick to anything long enough to make it habit-forming. But from hope springs eternal complacency. There's another shrink-wrapped cure right around the corner.

If my thoughts appear somewhat sarcastic, they are meant to be. My observations are meant to provoke, not offend. However, you may need to read between the lines to really get the message. My experiences are meant to initiate autopsies on what we've done and what we're doing. Why do baseball teams go to spring training? The boys and girls of spring practice their fundamentals.

Why do organizations continue to push on into more complex and sophisticated programs when they don't even know what the fundamentals are, let alone practice them? The "Here's Your Halos" included in this book contain many of the false hopes and expectations we've been feeding the workforce for lo these many years. Look on the shelves in the backroom and count the number of programs and initiatives that are simply iterations of the same theme. We shouldn't be shocked as leaders to know that the people we lead understand that the next "flavor of the month" will still taste like garbage. If they are patient this too shall pass, only to be replaced by more garbage.

I write like I talk and teach. So if you don't like this book- you are probably only one of many thousands of potential clients who have never hired me, and maybe never will. But that's okay, because there's a chance I couldn't work for you anyway. I'm not cynical, I'm knowledgeable- there's a difference. This book challenges people, places and things because managers, department heads, supervisors and owners pretending to be leaders are high risk to subordinates like my kids now old enough to enter the workforce. I'm taking it personally.

To get benefit from this book you must be open to critique, be driven to improve, embrace change, accept and even seek risks, and have a somewhat perverse sense of humor. I understand and embrace many of your management objectives. But if you don't balance your management objectives with leadership skills, I just don't want you filling up cemeteries with good or high potential employees in achieving them. If you don't enjoy the book, then possibly we both have wasted some valuable time. You also might be one of the people I don't want my kids working for.

Δ *If you're too big to be criticized, you're too small to be praised.*

Author unknown

Napkin Notes

- *Leadership is a Calling. Don't get into it for the wrong reasons.*
- *Why Do You Want to be a Leader?*
- *What Have You Done to Prepare Yourself for Leadership?*
- *Are You Doing It for You, or For Them?*
- *Leaders are Measured Around their Hearts. Managers are Measured Around their Heads*
- *Balance Task with Relationships*

Chapter 2: Leading the Roger Milliken Way

Picking the Fruit

The roots of my frustration probably started in the early 70's with personal experience on how committed leadership can run organizations, in of all places a dirty old cotton mill in Spartanburg, South Carolina. My first employer in the private sector- a somewhat secretive organization at the time called *Deering Milliken* (now simply *Milliken*) taught me many lessons about commitment and leadership.

Having worked on a swing shift in a cotton mill thirty five years ago taught me lessons you can't learn in a leadership lab at some university, or even observe it as an outside consultant. Those lessons, built upon over the years, enable me to Tell You What I Know, not What I Think.

Milliken's roots date back to 1865 when Seth Milliken and William Deering founded Deering Milliken Company, a small woolen fabrics company in Portland, Maine. Deering soon left to start his own company. You may have heard of it- John Deere.

Since Milliken has been a closely held private company since then, many of you may not be familiar with Roger Milliken, or what his company has achieved over the years. *Milliken* presently is ranked #16 in *Fortune's 100 Best Companies to Work For*. The company has over 1,900 patents for 36,000 different fabrics, yarn and chemical products. It is one of the only U.S. companies to achieve both the Malcolm Baldrige Quality Award and the Japan Institute of Plant Maintenance TPM Excellence Award.

It has the largest textile research center in the world, and management associates average 75 hours annually of extra educational training. Milliken University is internationally recognized as one of the most demanding training programs available. I've been to a lot of places and done many things with many companies since my tenure with Roger Milliken, but I remain fiercely proud of my experience as a cotton mill "Lint Head". And I wouldn't trade my cotton mill experiences for any others I can think of.

Many years ago, when Roger addressed me as part of a group of new hires, he said "As a new manager I don't expect you to give any orders to anyone for the first thirty days, unless you absolutely have to. Listen to your people, and ask them what to do". That advice was so wisely simple, I wrote it down. For me, that's advice that has stood the test of time, and contributed immensely to whatever success I've had in the leadership game.

When I go into an organization to straighten out management issues, the first people I talk to are the employees. They talk a different language, and they're holding onto the "organizational elephant" in an entirely different place than management is.

Back in the day there was no middle emotional ground if you worked for *Milliken*. Cotton Mill work back then was not for the "faint of heart". You either loved it or hated it. If you were in operations, you worked a forty-eight hour swing shift. If you were staff, you were still expected to put in a scheduled forty-eight hours.

Rewards were plentiful but punishment was swift and harsh if you couldn't "cut it". Labor disputes were occasionally "settled" out in the parking lot. You got respect from your employees only when you proved yourself worthy of it; not because someone had given you a fancy title like Manager.

As part of the labor force, your daddy and/or mama probably worked in the same mill doing the same job you had, and your work heritage could probably be traced back through several generations at the same location. To this day the old "mill village" concept of support and family remains alive and well. Even though for the most part old mill villages had long ago disappeared, the long held attitudes about "work family" and "going through it together" are still spiritual mantras that most folks in cotton mill country adhere to.

There are many reasons why unions don't waste their time in attempting to organize Milliken. There are reasons why poor leaders don't last long in an accountable environment. These are the same reasons that allowed Milliken to earn the Malcolm Baldrige award before it was fashionable.

- **Loyalty** When the famous gas shortages hit in the early 70's, the textile business was one of the hardest hit of all industries. As a relatively new trainee on probation, I fully expected to be released. The mill I worked at was totally shut down for a period of time. I was actually shocked to learn that because I had committed to the company, Milliken in return committed to keep me in the company if at all possible. I went from a supervisory trainee to a night watchman because there was no one at the time for me to supervise, but I kept my job and salary. My first big lesson in Company Loyalty. You can't buy loyalty; you got to give it to get it. Companies that "throw" money at people in order to keep the peace or keep unions out haven't learned this lesson yet.

  My people later on in my cotton mill career taught me about how loyalty is returned to a loyal employer. When a union organizer passed out handbills in front of my plant one morning, I found nine of my employees waiting for me in the office with the handbills in their hands and a smile on their faces. I'll never forget what they told me: "Look what these idiots are trying to do". These folks never had the need to seek out a third party to speak out for them. They knew if they had a problem, that management would listen carefully and <u>respectfully</u>, and try to fix the problem. There's no secret here. I have learned over the many years since then that "If you have a union, you deserve one". I am not anti-union. **I am** anti-bad management.

- **Thinking Outside the Box** Each year Roger Milliken spent thousands of dollars sending hundreds of management trainees to something called *Freedom School*, which was actually conducted by one of the founders of the <u>Libertarian Movement</u> (LaFerve). Roger Milliken was not a Libertarian, but he knew that spending four days being exposed to some fairly radical ideas would most certainly stimulate our thinking and emotions. And it did in spades. We learned absolutely nothing about the technical aspects of the textile industry, but we as trainees learned a lot about ourselves, our shared values and belief systems. And for some reason Mr. Milliken thought that was an important aspect of Leadership, and spent a lot of money in making it happen. That in and of itself is pretty damn radical, isn't it?

- **Process Training** Regardless of who you were, or at what level you were hired at, everyone went through the Management Orientation Program. (Remember this is thirty plus years ago). This orientation was a three week long program exposing us to the entire Critical Process, from the buying of cotton to the sales and marketing of finished products. "Silo Management" was unacceptable. You had to learn where stuff came from, and where it was supposed to go. From an early age we learned about and were held accountable for our Internal Customers and Suppliers. Just as important, or even more so, is the fact that the workforce was continuously trained in and held accountable for implementing Process Management techniques. Milliken knew that quality and service was not a product of an organization chart. People at all levels had to sell it, make it and deliver it for the customer to be satisfied.

Personal ownership went beyond process and service to areas such as teamwork and safety. One day I visited a Milliken plant dressed "to the nines". I looked and smelled like somebody important. I happened to go in a side door closest to the parking lot without my trusty pair of safety glasses. A lady immediately left her spinning frame and told me "Sir, I require that safety glasses be worn in my area, because I'm concerned about your safety". There weren't any large safety banners up, or blinking safety signs to remind her to do this. This was simply how she viewed her world and span of control. Even though she was "just a spinner", she was passionate about safety. When management shines a light on something as being important, people pay attention to it.

- **"Screw Up and Move** Up *OUT***"** Everyone in a leadership position, from plant managers to front line supervisors, were exposed to annual Morale Surveys (completed by direct and indirect reports), and Safety Audits among others. If you as a leader failed any of these audits, you were given immediate Corrective Action and training in your specific deficiency, and re-audited. If you failed the audit a second time, you packed your bags and left for greener, less accountable pastures with another company. Milliken was often described as "training ground" for other companies' executives. You weren't hidden, or transferred to another area where you might do less damage or kill (figuratively) fewer people. Poor leadership at any level was swiftly and effectively dealt with. Employees at the lowest levels of the organization knew they had a voice in the quality of their leadership and working environment. Having the opportunity to submit input and suggestions to management is one thing. Getting answers and seeing action based on your input is "putting your money where people's mouths are".

> Δ ***It's better to rise to your
> level of incompetence
> than being demoted to it.***
>
> Author unknown

Do They Even Know I'm Here?

Milliken's famous <u>Chart Room</u>, located at HQ in Spartanburg, SC was the answer to this question. In this room, organized by division, was a picture of every person in a management or leadership position, from General Managers through management trainees. On each individual picture was listed the respective training that person had received, dates of that training and purposed next steps for development.

For an entire week each year Roger Milliken sat with all his division heads, and went through the development potential of every person within that division head's span of control. And that Division Head had better do his/her homework. Each manager knew there would be personal follow up by "Big Red" and direct accountability if their plans for even the lowest of low on that chart were not completed.

As a young supervisor, I knew that no matter how large the organization was or how complex the chain of command, my work and development would receive due diligence from the highest levels of management.

If your organization contains two or more levels of leadership, and you have upward mobile people looking for the right career path, this becomes a major issue you may not even be aware of. Do you think there are people within your span of control who wonder how certain individuals are able to keep their jobs?

Maybe that's because no one beyond their immediate supervision is looking at their contributions, or lack thereof. Maybe managers living in the rarified air of senior leadership should take more than a cursory look at the overall development and accountability of their personnel.

Leading by Example

Early one morning in 1975 I was working in the Weave Room at Drayton Mill in Spartanburg with one of my Fixers (maintenance man) on a loom that was giving us fits. My Fixer's formal name was James Elliot, but folks who knew him called him "Slab". I happened to be wedged under the loom looking at stuff I knew absolutely nothing about, when I heard a voice from above say "Slab, how are they running tonight?" My first thought was "Who the hell is this?

And can't this idiot see they're not running worth a flip at two o'clock in the morning?" All I could see from my strategic position under this dirty old loom was a pair of old work boots and the bottom of work coveralls. I heard Slab reply the obvious "Roger, they're not running worth a damn tonight!"

Well, I'm thinking that maybe this guy named Roger could help us out. As I unwedged myself from under the loom, the owner of the boots and overalls began to materialize. With one arm around Slab's shoulder, Roger Milliken extended his other hand to help me up.

To a young supervisor, like myself, this was like God himself extending his hand to me. This multi-multi millionaire, direct owner of over seventy plants worldwide, was helping me off the floor at two o'clock in the morning. Roger spent about an hour with Slab and me, talking about everything from the high humidity that affected how the looms ran, to reminiscing about some recent retirees he and Slab both knew. I found out later that Mr. Milliken was a frequent visitor to all his plants, unannounced and without fanfare. Just to see how things were going and how "his people" were doing.

Δ *It takes two to see the truth-one to speak and the other to hear.*

Henry David Thoreau

Right or wrong, I've been trying to get organizations to pay attention to my hard-earned lessons for the past thirty years. Roger Milliken (or 'Big Red' as he was known to us peons in the trenches) to this day serves as a model for leaders who have a sense of the necessary balance between task and relationship.

He had his faults, but totally committing his money and resources to what he thought best for both his customers' requirements and the workforce responsible for meeting those requirements are not on the list. Roger created an organization in which not everyone could work.

You either loved him or hated him. Milliken was known as the training ground for future executives for other textile companies. He spent a lot of money weeding people out that couldn't work in his highly accountable environment. He made a lot of money weeding these people out as well.

I am using thirty year old stories as a part of this book's basic premise. We don't "Practice What We Preach". Hell, we don't even "Walk the Talk". We don't need a lot of new skills or fancy workshops to remind us about the attributes of a true leader. If you are an experienced manager, "rediscover" the passion of leadership.

If you are a newly minted manager or supervisor, listen to your people and the voices of those who have led before you. And ***Resist*** being influenced by "Politically Correct" training, books and mentors. From a leadership standpoint, your biggest challenges will come from ***Politically Incorrect*** people. You better learn how to deal with them at their level.

Δ *You'll only be as good as you allow your people to be.*

Tom Fehlman

Napkin Notes

- *Never Walk Past People Doing a Good Job*
- *Benchmark Against Recognized Leaders*
- *Do Your People Feel "Ownership of Their Jobs?*
- *Don't Ask Questions if You Do Nothing With the Answers*
- *Allow People to Think Creatively*
- *Integrate People into the Entire Process*
- *When You Shine a Light on It, People Will Pay Attention*
- *You got to Give Loyalty to Get It*

Chapter 3: What We Have Here is a Failure to Commune

It is time for us to sit back, reflect on our past sins and missed opportunities, and move to higher and more passionate elevations of leadership. We get so involved in the mundane tasks of management; we forget the spiritual aspects of leadership. We need some type of "cosmic enema" to clean out all the false leadership crap and scar tissue we've absorbed over the years. Leadership is much more of a calling than it is a job.

Some of you have it; others are looking for it. Some of you have twenty years of leadership experience; others have one year of experience twenty times. Some of you know when you "step in it"; some have no idea their leadership techniques are somewhat odorous. Some of you walk toward the light; others live on the "dark side".

If you lead people for your benefit, and not theirs --- the messages contained within will call you to task. If you are in the leadership game for power, fame and glory, or if you savor even small victories, enjoy producing with productive people, and are driven to make positive differences with occasionally negative people; be "Fruitful and Multiply".

Out of the 7000 plus assessments I've conducted in the past twenty-five years, fully half of them involved technically oriented people who learned technical stuff from their parents, went to school to be engineers or technicians, and actually took technically oriented jobs because they actually enjoyed the stuff! They are binary thinkers who do not see a need to move from their absolute right-wrong views of world. More power to them.

We need folks like this; just not in leadership roles. At the same time I need to recognize those technically oriented, left brain managers who have identified their strengths and liabilities, and are working hard to expand their leadership skill base. I would rather assess people with no skills but have an interest and aptitude to learn about leadership, than assess a half-baked, half-ass technocrat who believes he/she is fulfilling some type of management prophecy. Stick to what you like or love to do!

"I'm Too Busy"

I've seen cats being "busy" in a cat box. No matter how hard they work at covering things up, their process never seems to improve. I know the story. When you've finished one pile on the desk; three more piles have taken its place. There is always work to be done. I believe work gets done better when you're ready to do it.

Sometimes you have to take time to go to the mountaintop, and commune with the Why's and Wherefores of Leadership. Take a breath, kick a can, and step away from your binary thinking for a minute or two. Maybe even read a book on what you're supposed to be doing, rather than working so hard to prove what you're presently doing is right. Define if you can differences between you the Manager and you the Leader.

Recently I was asked by a client to resolve both process and personnel issues between and among two separate departments and the union. Evidently there was constant bickering over the use of common resources such as overhead cranes, and because business was rapidly expanding within one department, they were constantly drawing on the use of resources and personnel from the other department.

To make matters worse, because the rapidly expanding department was undermanned, the people they were borrowing from the other areas were often asked to work up to eighty <u>days</u> straight without any time off, on twelve hour shifts. My own personal response to the work hours was that if they didn't already have a union, they deserved to have one. People resisted being transferred to this department, and the union understood the production needs, was caught in the middle because of the resistance and resentment of their rank and file in being transferred to "the department from hell".

In the recently completed contract talks, in addition to the ridiculous work hours, the union also complained that employees being transferred to the high intensity department were being "used and abused"; to the point people didn't want to go there to work just normal hours. When I asked the respective department head about these charges his reply was "I'm here to get the work out, and some people don't appreciate it".

When I asked him about a particular supervisor who was being singled out as being the most abusive his reply was not surprising but equally dismaying. "I brought this guy with me when I transferred here, and I trust him to get the work out". The department head had been through my assessment process two years earlier, and had been assessed being, among other things, reactive and task driven.

He had then gone through my leadership training program, which prompted me to ask where his Leadership "Cue Cards" were. He pointed them out as being somewhere on the bottom shelf under a pile of books. By this time he had my full attention, which I ensured he felt. When I asked him why he wasn't using his leadership skills he completed the TriFecta by answering "I'm too busy getting work out".

I have heard somewhere that diplomacy was defined as "telling someone to go to hell in such a way they looked forward to the trip". I'm afraid I was not that diplomatic in pointing out that he and his supervision were actually limiting production by being "bosses". His group didn't have the time <u>not to be leaders</u>! To make matters worse, at times he was actually going behind his co-mangers' backs to the big boss to get what he wanted. His own mother wouldn't trust him at this point.

The day after I got back home from this frustrating and exhausting trip, I received an email from this manger outlining the set of Leadership Skills I wanted him to use, and his commitment to begin coaching these skills to his managers immediately. He also told me he had already gone to his co-managers and personally apologized to them about his misguided passion.

The kicker is that when I went to this manger's HR resource to review his assessment report, the HR Manager revealed to me somewhat hesitantly that the report was still in his inbox, and had been there for <u>two years.</u> There had obviously been no follow up, accountability or reinforcement for this guy since he had been trained. Truth is stranger than fiction, and I almost wished he had lied to me.

My work at this location has obviously just begun. Everyone at this location in a management position shares complicity in what I view as a "crime against the people". No one trusts anyone here, and is it any wonder? The first thing I told corporate was that I wasn't charging them enough to do this work. The second thing I told them was that they needed to be ready to make wholesale management changes at this location if I couldn't get it straightened out. They needed to start at the very top.

Δ If you go fast enough, you may overtake whatever you're trying to escape from.

Author unknown

What Is It All About Alfie?

How many of us are promoted to a management role before we feel we're ready? If a management role is what we are striving for, how many of us have actually prepared ourselves for such a role? We do not set out with questions about leadership; we look for others to give us answers about leadership. This is a recipe for disaster. Why?

Because Leadership is about Relationships. How many relationships are you aware of that are 100% predictable 100% of the time? I have yet to read a book or attend any worthwhile leadership workshop that promises precisely "right and wrong" answers to leadership issues. Managers manage tasks, and Leaders lead Behavior.

Other than a relationship with who's now an ex-wife, I'm not aware of any fully predictable behaviors. (Odds go up if we are talking about teenagers, who are **100%** unpredictable). Ask questions before you get into Leadership. And Never Stop! Someone very wise once said that our job as leaders is to "Answer questions and question answers". Read any book or attend any workshop you can find that addresses Behavior Modification. (Unfortunately there aren't that many around!) Just understand that Alfie doesn't have any absolute answers for you. And neither does this book.

> *Δ I'm not ready for the future, but fortunately it hasn't yet arrived.*

> Ashleigh Brilliant

Inheritance Tax

What gives us the right to think we got rights? Leadership is not something we deserve because of seniority, or success at doing our tasks. Leadership is an ethical, moral and skillful position we must earn. We must care not only about what is done, but <u>how</u> it is done by others. Show me a young Accountant who's been running numbers for five years, and I'll show you a Leader in Waiting for their turn to be promoted to a Leader Position.

I'll also lay you odds that they haven't read a leadership book or taken a management course on their own initiative in those five years. Promotion by Entitlement is still a malady and common disease which remains untreatable by many organizations. And the people that suffer most under this philosophy are the folks who must work in it. What a crappy existence! How dare we accuse our people of having no initiative when we're not engaging in it ourselves.

> *Δ A promotion is a sign that either you're doing something right, or your boss just did something wrong.*

> Author unknown

Napkin Notes

- *Are You Using the Skills You've Already Been Trained In?*
- *Answer Questions and Question Answers*
- *In Leadership, It's Better to be Approximately Right than Precisely Wrong!*
- *Have a Clear Vision of what Your Want to Look Like as a Leader*
- *Think as a Behaviorist. Get some Behavior Modification Training*
- *Stick to What You Like to Do*

Chapter 4: Leaders Are Born, Not Bred

Leadership vs Management

Natural leaders are mission specific. Patton could not have been Gandhi, and vice versa. Mother Theresa could not have led the Sioux against Custer, and so on, and so on. Give me someone who wants to learn how to lead, and unless they have some serious flaw in their style makeup, I can teach them how to survive as a leader.

What really quivers my liver, about leadership and the lip service we give it, is that organizations large and small have really yet to define it in terms of what leadership should look like for their cultures, customers and workforce. I will grant you that many organizations include leadership competencies in their Performance Appraisal programs, which someone once defined as "given by someone who doesn't want to give them, to someone who doesn't want to get them."

I **have not seen** many managers held fully accountable for their leadership applications until they reach "serial killer" status. However, if a manager completes tasks on schedule I'll guarantee you it doesn't matter how many cemeteries he/she fills up on the way to victory. Good producers don't necessarily or automatically make good leaders. Good Leadership skills that produce through the efforts of others make Good Leaders.

I've been asking the same company for ten years what their supervisors look like from a leadership skill standpoint, and for ten years that question has been met with eerie silence. Because we wait for "natural" leaders to emerge from wherever they come from, we spend little time and even less resources actually preparing potential leaders for positions before they are needed.

We put them in open positions <u>now</u> and hope they survive until they get the training they need that they won't be held accountable for using anyway. What we end up with is like wetting your pants: it feels warm at first and then it gets cold real quick.

He/She is a good sales person; let's promote him/her to sales manager. Unfortunately this phenomenon happens in all organizations, at all levels, and all the time. Guess what, Snoopy. Leadership skill sets are much different than tool grinder skill sets, or selling skill sets, or accounting skill sets for that matter. There is more than enough blame to go around, however. We want our leaders to show initiative.

How many of your present managers or supervisors actually began preparing themselves for leadership before stepping "into the breach"? It's amazing to me that people prepare themselves to run jobs, but do not prepare themselves to become leaders if that indeed is on their radar scope. Stop sending potential leaders into battle unarmed! It wastes your time and theirs, and annoys the hell out of the people they are supposed to be leading.

The MBA Syndrome

May the saints protect us from MBAs! An MBA is to leadership as Richard Simmons is to pro wrestling. At best an MBA may give them exposure to leadership theory, and they may even do some role playing for demonstration purposes. But they teach little in the way of practical application of leadership skills at 3:00 a.m. when a supervisor has three open jobs because he/she has some severe attendance issues on their shift.

How do I know? Because I have personally conducted over 7000 Leadership Assessment Centers, and many MBA graduates I've assessed possess an arrogance and self assuredness that quickly disappears when I put them "on the firing line."

Advanced degrees are good and even necessary in today's macro business climate. They prepare people well for managing the tasks of the business.

But they don't give a graduate "*street cred*" in terms of motivating "Walk on Water's, or leading "Seeds of Satan".

Regardless of whether your organization is large or small; in service or manufacturing; put some type of leadership apprenticeship or evaluative process in place before you turn these people loose. My kids will eat them up if these so-called graduates don't have some well defined leadership skills in place.

Corporate Favoritism

"Our management really likes him/her!" Of course they like people who deliver on time and within budget. And everybody loves producers. Who doesn't? The question is, Are people going through walls for their leaders, or are managers pushing their people through walls? If our workforce is paying the price to meet customer requirements, how much more can they stand to pay? When managers have enough power, they obviously can force issues. But force is only a small part of the makeup of the modern leader.

If you think you're the leader, look back once in a while to see if anyone is following you. A Game Warden in Arizona once told me, "If it's your job to lead the herd, occasionally you'd better look back to see if the herd is behind you". Organizations do not spend enough time sorting out internal customer/supplier relationships and accountabilities.

We <u>do</u> spend a lot of time ensuring our "org" charts are current and up to date. I have yet to see an organization chart that truly reflects working relationships and accountabilities. To a large degree, I believe the person who last touches it before delivery to the customer, is actually often <u>the most important </u>person in the process. When managers view themselves, and are themselves viewed as *suppliers* to their people, rather than the "boss" of them, the whole leadership dynamic changes.

Ain't My Job

Guess what? Somebody's gotta do it! Holding people accountable seems to be that fella's job who is hiding behind the tree. Many years ago I was exposed to the "DO Brothers" from an old mentor and training sage named Al Sivewright. I have used the simile many times since in my training and consulting. I use it frequently because the need to issue "wake up" calls is frequent. The "DO Brothers" can be treated as a consistent axiom. It goes as follows:

1. <u>Could Do</u> Human Resources and the Hiring Authority ensures that the candidate *could* do the work.

2. <u>Can Do</u> Training Resources ensures the employee *can* do the work.

3. <u>Will Do</u> The Leader ensures the employee *will* do the work.

The three brothers are "All in the Family". It is a tight knit family that depends on each other. The *buck* doesn't stop until <u>all three brothers</u> have been met. Good Leaders ensure all three conditions are in place. They don't blame Human Resources for hiring poor candidates. They don't blame Human Resources for lack of support.

And, they don't blame Training for providing them poorly skilled employees. Good Leaders take responsibility for the entire process. Poor Leaders "pass the buck" from one brother to the other. They end up with employees who have literally "retired on the Job" because they place blame on others for their failure to lead, or simply fail to confront because that can be unpleasant.

Δ "He Ain't Heavy, He's My brother"

Napkin Notes

- *Remember the "DO" Brothers*
- *The Best Producers don't always make Good Leaders or Coaches*
- *The Last person to Touch It May be the Most Important Person in the Process*
- *Don't Confuse an MBA with Practical Leadership Skills*
- *Sometimes You Have to be Patton, Sometimes You Have to be Gandhi*
- *Good Leaders Take Responsibility for the Entire Process*
- *You are an Internal Supplier to the People Who work for You*
- *If You're the Leader, Make Sure the Herd is Still Behind You.*
- *Good Leaders Don't Get "Fragged" by Their Own Troops*

Chapter 5: Training is Important

Are you kidding me? Throw a task our way, and watch how quickly training programs fade into black. When the market shrinks, competition increases or resources become scarce; training is often the first area to get cut. There are only several ways to increase skill level in the marketplace, and training/retraining are the key components to improvement and competitiveness. (See Figure *Sink of Skill*).

The ironic part of this story is that people that need training the most; people who last touch the product, or have direct contact with customers in the field, are the people voted least likely to get the training they need.

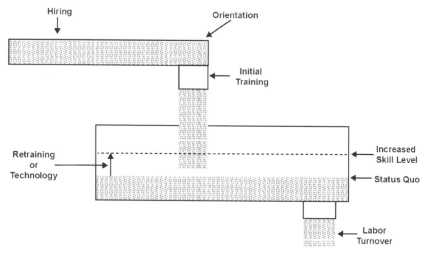

We Don't Have the Time Right Now

We can't free him or her up, or there are meetings to attend, or we can't bring them in from the field right now, or whatever. Isn't it strange that the people at whom training is often directed are the best in figuring out how to get out of it? You know the old line "I don't have time to go to a Time Management workshop now". They are not held responsible for getting it, nor are their managers for ensuring they get it. For a pig, bacon and eggs means total commitment.

People are called out of workshops; are late from breaks being tied up on the bane of trainers-the cell phone, or simply choose not to even show up. When these people go on vacation I assume the entire organization shuts down. If we don't train simply for the sake of training, then training should be committed to, and closely tied to process or people improvement.

Occasionally we might even consider making some worthy leadership courses required training, or at least required reading. From a strategic standpoint targeted training needs to become non negotiable.

Δ Figure out what needs to be trained and train it-No Exceptions

Tom Fehlman

I Already Have Experience

What a joke! More often than not those sixteen years of experience is simply one year of experience they've had sixteen times. Why do we buy off on the notion that experience equals skill? The mantel of "Experience" allows people to walk unencumbered through the doors of new hires, and allows incumbents to continue unhindered cutting swaths through entire workforces.

Why doesn't senior leadership require proof of the "right stuff" of leadership? Because poor leadership based on experience is easier to allow or avoid confronting, than *requiring* training from experienced managers who already believe they have all the answers. As an old "lint head" trainer of some thirty plus years, the best challenges I get these days are those narrow-minded idiots who say, "I don't need it; I'm an experienced manager". They usually don't know crap about leadership, and what they did know is so covered up by scar tissue they can't find it anymore. Are you Reactive or Proactive?

Δ If Training is Optional;
then Results are
Optional.

Tom Fehlman

They Have Already Been Trained

Show me someone who has been trained as lately as two days ago, and I will show you someone who is not doing what they've been trained to do. I compare this phenomena somewhat to buying something because it's on sale; not because you need it, or ever have any intention of using it. I've actually been told by training managers that "we don't want to use you too much because we want to avoid repetition".

Yet we know that for the most part folks only effectively process about 25% of what they hear in a ten minute lecture. I'm still looking for a study which validates that two months later participants are still applying 75% of what they learned in a leadership workshop. If they're not actually applying most of what they've learned, why did we put them through the damn workshop in the first place? If it's important, it bares repeating, over and over and over.

And, to compound matters, when participants get trained they are often sent back to managers who have no idea what they've been trained in; therefore, incapable of supporting, nurturing or coaching needed applications. Managers desperately need to know what is being offered as training for their people, whether or not it has value and application so they can at least attempt to reinforce and/or hold accountable their subordinates for applying the skills.

Δ *If you want skill or cultural changes- Make It Habit Forming*

Tom Fehlman

Sit by Nellie

In my old cotton mill days, we had a saying that "If you sit by Nellie long enough, you will figure out what Nellie is doing." It doesn't make much sense, so why do we do it? Because people can run a job well, does not mean they can train well. Worse yet, people who are doing the training may actually not enjoy it, which means trainees may come out of the training experience having little skills but one helluva attitude.

If you have people being trained right now, I'll bet you my last bottle of Henrietta's Malt Liquor that whoever is training them is focused on producing their task, not on training their understudies. Unless **Trainer Criteria** is set up to actually qualify who may instruct and teach, the risk is high that employees who do not have skill transfer as their main driver will not do adequate jobs as trainers.

Good Mentors, Coaches and even OJT Instructors do not come by their skills by accident. They have been trained to transfer skill, and both they and their students are given time enough to complete that transfer. Some of my best battles have been fought with operations people who are eager to move people into skill positions because they are upright and fog up a mirror. Why must our people learn through the acquisition of scar tissue?

At a higher level, so-called sophisticated companies still rush inexperienced, untested and unseasoned youngsters into the breach, because they got degrees and, by the way, they happen to be damn good engineers. I don't want my kids working for these people. Do you?

Δ *Training at all levels should occur by Design; not by Accident*

Tom Fehlman

We Invest in Training

Who Are You Fooling? "Join Our Fast-Paced Company" means "Fool, we're moving so fast we have no time to train you." Many organizations view training monies as "discretionary" spending which has little if anything to do with true investment. Guess what first gets cut if the marketplace puts on a little pressure?

I submit to you if companies were actually serious and committed to training the right skills at the right time, they would not have to worry so much about the whims and foibles of the marketplace. And if spending money on training *hurts* like a real investment, exactly what do you expect as a Return on that Investment?

How many companies actually follow up with and hold accountable participants for using the skills they just received from a leadership training class? You might get a general question such as "Did you enjoy it? Or a vague question such as "Did you get anything out of it? but that's usually where the questioning and accountability stops.

What usually dictates your training budget is last year's training budget, and how much of it got used before the end of the fiscal year. How many times have training budgets ended up with surplus at the end, which creates a rush to spend it so we don't lose it? I know this because as a Training Manager for a large international company I had this type of pressure applied to me on an annual basis.

The old adage "If you think training is expensive, consider ignorance" applies here with some slight modification. Training needs and respective expenditures are usually determined by silo owners and turf battles, not by true process owners who truly understand the needs of the process as determined by customer requirements. Training needs to be thought of in Strategic terms, not just from a tactical view.

Δ *If you think Training is expensive; consider Ignorance.*

Tom Fehlman

I Believe in the Value of Training

This is a well intended Myth that just doesn't hold much water. The proof is all around us. Training is okay when there's nothing else to do. The proof is also in the individual and composite Psychometric Profiles I create during my assessment process. It is amazing to me how many people aspiring to be leaders score "below the Mendoza line" in the area of Interest in Self Development.

These people are self delusional. Do I really expect them to develop my kids when they have spent little to no effort in developing themselves for a leadership role? I love the (possibly Chinese) proverb which states "Starving Man Wait Long Time for Roast Duck to Fly in Mouth". Surely an old trainer type came up with this one. We have a lot of people *waiting* for the organization to train them.

We wonder why our leaders don't show more initiative or risk taking. Maybe we should start by looking at how much initiative they've shown in developing themselves for leadership positions. If they didn't have it then, they sure as hell won't have it now. Wasn't it Mark Twain who said?

Δ "*I'll learn 'em or I'll kill 'em*".

Mark Twain

Napkin Notes

- *Don't Mistake Experience for Skill Level*
- *Leadership is a Continuous Process*
- *If You think Training is Expensive, Consider the Cost of Ignorance*
- *Train and Re-Train to Make Skills Habit-Forming*
- *Don't Confuse OJT with "Sit by Nellie" experiences*
- *Good Trainers have been Taught How to Transfer Skills*
- *Management Should Know and be Able to Reinforce Subordinate Training*
- *Hold Employees Accountable for the Training They Receive*
- *Memorize the Sink of Skill*

Chapter 6: Six Sigma

As the title suggests, the latest quality improvement programs such as Six Sigma are simply the latest iteration of processes going back forty years. Let's see; we've had in varying order Quality Circles, Total Quality Management, Process Management, JIT (Just in Time), Statistical Process Control, Lean Manufacturing, Balanced Scorecard, Throughput Accounting, Constraint Management, Synchronous Flow among others.

All are fancy reiterations of the same theme addressing business transformation and the impacts on organizational capability and effectiveness. Hey, unless you understand the fundamentals of change management and the best way to sustain the solution under the current business climate…you're right back where we all started.

Twenty-five years ago I assisted Japanese companies such as Honda (Burlington, NC) implement Quality Circles in their American plants because of cultural differences. This was one of my first experiences with cultural differences between company to company, and even from one workplace to another in the same company. What works well in one environment may create chaos in another. Most certainly it will create confusion.

I am a trained facilitator and implementer of programs designed by J.M. Juran, SPC (Statistical Process Control) and Edward Deming. I am presently engaged in learning the intricacies of Synchronous Flow based on Theory of Constraints made popular by Goldratt way back in the early 1980s.

Interestingly, Synchronous Flow is also a composite of the best offered by Lean Manufacturing, Throughput Accounting, and Six Sigma among others. A large international company I work with has been training Six Sigma and *Belts* of all colors for the past five years. This is a huge investment of time and money.

When you go out on the floor where people are either putting quality in or taking it out, if you ask them about <u>Six</u> Sigma they look at you like you're a side dish they didn't order. *Balanced Scorecards* is another example of a shrink wrapped package gone horribly awry. And the beat goes on.

All this by way of asking *"Why don't you make what you already got work?"* Know this for sure-None of these Flavors of the Month will work in "Silo Management" where the core and critical support processes have not been identified and measured. How many Flavors do you have on the shelf gathering dust?

Δ *If your Silos work, your Processes probably don't.*

Tom Fehlman

High-Priced Consultants Are the Way to Go

Two union avoidance campaigns I've been involved with in the past several years were necessitated by one of the "Big Three" consulting firms and their stuffed suits. They attempted to shove Lean Manufacturing down a workforce's throat with no regard to how the workforce felt about it. *Getting all the people to go in one direction also describes a mutiny.* How does it work?

They come to visit you with their experienced lead people; impress the hell out of you with their PowerPoint© presentations; secure a high priced long-term contract; and use second and third tier people to implement their "shrink wrapped" packages. In my experienced opinion, the irony is that the high-priced packages work the worse <u>for the simplest solutions that should call for the least cost.</u>

The big consulting groups (and some not so big) of this world charge big bucks and therefore feel strong ownership of their methods, and their second and third tier consultants have little to no experience in implementing anything but the program as it is packaged. You don't believe me!

Hire a high-priced consultant to conduct a Creative Thinking workshop for you, and see how much variation there is in their shrink-wrapped presentation. And if they offer to come in beforehand to determine what the needs really are <u>at no cost to you</u>, please let me know!

Δ Don't pay highly placed vegetables to pick low hanging fruit.

Tom Fehlman

We've Got to Stay Current

This mentality is tied directly to the Flavor of the Month Club mentioned above, but it's the attitude that makes this comment stink, not the way we deal with it. Are we trying to keep up with our competition, or get ahead of them? There is merit in gaining competitive advantages, but when we build progress upon shaky foundations we will barely maintain status quo, let alone stay current.

New programs or advanced technology can simply be the exchange of one nuisance for another. One company I consulted with twenty years ago stated that communication was their biggest barrier to success. Upon a recent visit to the same company I asked the same questions, and got the same answers. For instance, "Is it better to do more less effectively, or do less more effectively?"

It's amazing to me that many organizations choose immediate gratification by doing more or less effectively, and end up losing customers in the long run. No matter how many veterans are on the team, baseball clubs undergo spring training every year to practice the basics and fundamentals of the game.

In the Leadership game, basics such as communication currencies, line of sight to customers, trust levels between and among management and the workforce, shared values and common objectives are the basic building blocks of progress.

No amount of current or future technologies can replace them. Once your basic task and leadership skills are static at a high level, by all means dive into the latest fad. Don't be fooled by the latest gimmick, or buy the newest iteration on the importance of Communication Skills because it comes in a new flavor. Don't do things differently because you need to change them.

Do things differently because they need to be changed. Benchmarking works only if you are going to use it to figure out how to make it better. If you don't believe me, ask the Japanese and more recently the Chinese and Indians. They don't use Benchmarking anymore to catch up. They use it to get ahead.

> *Δ Revisit your*
> *fundamentals, and don't*
> *leave home without them.*
>
> Tom Fehlman

We Are Customer Driven

Time to Flush this one out! Jim Belasco and Ralph Stayer in their book *Flight of the Buffalo* talk about **line of sight.** Everyone should have direct line of sight to external customers. I agree in theory, but it may not always be practical or cost effective. For sure is the fact that everyone in the organization needs to understand what the external customer drivers are, and <u>at the very least</u> have direct line of sight to their internal customers.

Back in my old cotton mill days, we were experiencing high off quality from our weave room. It was a classic case of *GIGO* (Garbage In, Garbage Out). Our weavers were contending with shoddy yarn coming from the Spinning Room. We begged, pleaded and threatened our spinners to produce better yarn for our Weave Room. Nothing changed; in fact it got worse; until we had our spinners follow our weavers around to looms that were being shut down because of poor yarn.

Weavers were losing incentive money because of the inattention of spinners to the quality of yarn they were producing. Weavers wasted no time in making their point to the spinners responsible. Buddy, we had ourselves a turnaround that would make your eyes see double. All Employees should be evaluated by internal and external customers; both at best and by internal customers at the very least.

Δ *The most important body in*
the process is the last one to touch it.

Tom Fehlman

Napkin Notes

- *Conduct After Action Reviews on Past Failed Programs*
- *Is It Better to Do More Less Effectively, or Do Less More Effectively?*
- *Everyone Should Have Direct Line of sight to an Internal or External Customer*
- *Customers Should Have Input into Individual Performance Reviews*
- *Don't Build on Faulty Fundamentals*
- *The Best Solutions are Often the Simplest Ones that Cost Less*
- *Beware of High-Priced Consultants with Shrink-Wrapped Packages*
- *How Many of Your People Know and Understand Your Mission Statement?*
- *Comprehensive Programs don't Work Well in Silo Management*

Chapter 7: Change You Before You Change Them

We may not be able to avoid change, but we definitely need to change the way we implement change. Most of the Change Initiatives I've observed could turn the stomachs of a herd of camels. We get all excited about the promised benefits of a new program and can't wait to push it "out of the hangar". Unfortunately, most of the time when we push it, it falls over a cliff! We get ready for new processes without getting our people ready who must manage and operate the new processes.

My first management encounter with change occurred in the formative years of my "cotton mill" days. As a new supervisor, I was placed on a management team charged with old, dirty, relatively inefficient Draper looms with brand new "Water Jet" looms. These new looms were clean, efficient, and much safer to operate than the old Draper looms.

In fact, they ran so much better than our old looms that weavers who operated the new water jet looms could make more incentive money on the new machinery. The workplace environment was also being remodeled to receive the Water Jets. New flooring and better lighting were all part of the Change Initiative. We were so excited for our weavers we evidently forgot to ask them about how they felt about the new workplace.

Our best, most experienced weaver was Bertha Mabry. She had operated the same set of about twenty of the old Draper looms over in a dingy, corner of the Weaveroom for about eighteen years. She was respected by all who knew her for her hard work and weaving expertise. Bertha was slated to be the first to move over into the new, clean environment, where there was no doubt in our mind, she would be thrilled to be working and making more money.

We on the management team were shocked beyond belief when she verbally and physically resisted moving, when all the hard data we thought we had pointed to an exciting and beneficial transition for everyone.

People Resist Change

It's a copout to dismiss Bertha's behavior as "People resist change". Resistance is a Symptom of behavior, not a Cause. Of course, our naïve, process-oriented Implementation Team never even considered resistance, let alone what might cause it. Once we got over our shock of Bertha's resistance to an outstanding management initiative, the reasons for that resistance became apparent.

(1) **Shock:** she never knew about the change and her involvement in it; (2) **Fear:** she would have to learn new techniques and, maybe most importantly (3) **Credibility:** her reputation over 18 years had been built upon how well she ran those old looms. No one could run those particular looms as well as Bertha could. Now she was being thrown back into "remix" and the general population.

The Cycle of Change has been described in many ways, but experienced by all of us in fairly common cycles. It will happen with the death of a loved one, or trading in that special car, or moving from a single (me) to a married (we) state. It happens in the workplace when we change jobs, or experience layoffs as either the survivor or the one laid-off. It occurs when we move into a team, or cross-train into new skills and jobs.

Ending My Grandpa Black once told me "Never let go of something unless you got ahold of something else". (He also told me never to name a pig I planned on eating, which I also believe to be words you can live by). **Ending** is when we have to let go of what is familiar and comfortable for us, without really knowing what is ahead. It is in fact Grieving a Loss.

Neutral is CHAOS. We have let go of the old and familiar, but we haven't yet grasped new skills or knowledge. **Neutral** in many ways is the scariest state to be in, without direction or foundation. We are Consciously Incompetent. We know what's ahead, but we don't know to deal with it.

Beginning is when we start to "get it". When the new day brings more excitement than fear. This is the state of mind where our comfort level begins to take root and grow. Our "Flight or Fight" instincts become much more realistic as to what really is taking place, and the drama of change begins to diminish.

Stop Signs on the Slippery Slope

Don't let new techniques overwhelm old, established ways too quickly. Take that Process Critical Path and benchmark it with time-sensitive Activities and Communication venues to prepare the workforce to swallow the change in appropriate doses. Bring your employees along on the Change Journey. Get them involved early in the Whys and the Wherefores of the change.

I absolutely embrace the notion that employees should never be surprised by what lies ahead of them. It works that way when disciplining, and it works that way when implementing. People can much easier digest negative impact when they know it's coming.

Present the reasons and rationale for change in cultural language and WIFMs (*What's In It for Me*). Impact on EBIT means nothing to someone running a machine or digging a ditch. Tell me about overtime or job security. And SELL ME on the need for Change. Forcing Change down my throat will create nothing but a gag reflex. Remember, you can't hold me accountable unless the Laws of Accountability have been met.

Laws of Accountability

1. **I must know what I'm supposed to do**

2. **I must know how to do it.**

3. **It must be within my personal control to do it**

4. **You must give me <u>specific feedback</u> on where I'm at, and where I need to be.**

The Laws are a two-bladed sword. If the organization and/or leaders have not met the Laws, then Accountability is not appropriate. If the Laws have been met, people must be held Accountable.

Another ingredient in the Change Mix is the unfolding dynamics of generational drivers. In his new book "[2]<u>Motivating the "What's In It for Me" Workforce</u> Cam Marston points out that today's workplace contains multiple generations with significant and different generational drivers. Baby Boomers crave structure, while the New Millennial workers seek personal freedom with short term goals.

Change programs must be flexible and subject to *change*, based on group and individual needs. However, never lose sight that at the end of the day, your goal may well be to create an organization in which not everyone can work. A well thought-out change program involves both Tasks and Activities; a balance between *Task* and *Relationships*.

One of the most potentially damaging tools ever invented by man is the old "Critical Path". You've seen these fancy "line on bubble" schematics that take a process from Point A to Point D, with algebraic equations for figuring out timelines, lag times and so on and so on. Each Critical Step often has supporting steps, all to be accomplished within a certain timeframe.

If one step encounters difficulties, it has a ripple effect on all consequential steps in the process. Unfortunately, I have very seldom seen a parallel "People" Critical Path, which takes people moving from Point A to Point D. Critical Paths also have "Ripple Effects" on the people walking the path.

---

2   Cam Marston <u>Motivating the "What's In It for Me" Workforce</u> (John Wiley & Sons, 2007)

Not too long ago I was involved with a client whose business had literally doubled almost overnight. Sales had increased dramatically. The population of the plant had to double to keep pace with the new business. Unfortunately, that meant that about one-half of the plant population was untrained. In their wisdom, plant management placed most of these new folks on the weekend shifts, under relatively inexperienced supervision.

Unfortunately, production didn't double, but off quality, waste and warranty work did. My suggestion, after the fact, was that we can only produce what our people are capable of producing. If you lose customers by producing and/or increasing poor quality, what good does it do to create more business to lose? I have heard consultants like myself described as "hiring a plane spotter the day after Pearl Harbor".

Getting the business and then figuring out how to do it works at times for small startup companies, but very seldom works for larger, more inflexible organizations. This was a case in point. Sometimes you have to take short term hits to get long term results.

Changes in processes must work in tandem with changes in leadership and workforce skill level. There are times that taking a hit tactically in the short term is necessary for long term success. When a business outgrows its ability to meet customer requirements, it is doomed both tactically and strategically unless we fall back to regroup.

I recently encountered a wise director of a field service company who told me he had to turn down $3 million of new business last year because he didn't have enough trained people to meet the increased load. Ron Macklin, you made my Christmas List this year! Let's bottle your wisdom and sell it to anyone who will buy it.

Napkin Notes

- *Don't Extend Your Business Beyond Your Capabilities*
- *Prepare People for Change before Implementing It*
- *People Change for Different Reasons, or "WIFMs"*
- *Resistance to Change is a Symptom; Not a Cause*
- *Include Generational "Drivers" in Your Planning*
- *Integrate People into the Change Process*
- *Apply the Laws of Accountability, which are non negotiable.*
- *Create an Organization in Which Not Everyone Can Work.*

Chapter 8: Our Processes are Engineered to Standard

When we dig deeper, this Dogma don't Hunt! Those of us who work in the business process management arena, where process re-engineering is _____, there are four-(4) general rules of thumb with identifying what standards to re-engineer:

#1) Some standards are not possible to achieve or no longer apply from the viewpoint of people that have to do them. When the best you have can't meet the standard, possibly the standard should be reviewed.

#2) People who do the job are seldom, if ever, included where they need to be in determining standards. It really frosts my petunias when an employee actually doing the job tells me, "Nobody ever asked". This usually means they have also found a knack for performing a task that is not documented anywhere.

#3) Processes are seldom geared to customer requirements in the first place. If they were, what would we ever do with those lovely organizational charts the administrative assistants spend so much time keeping updated? Many organizations are still organized by "silo" requirements; not driven by customer requirements. Some folks, including myself, believe that the last person to touch it before it gets to the customer <u>may actually</u> be the most important person in the process.

#4) The fact that standards are inconsistently supported by Best Practice Method procedures and standardized training, suggest that there remains huge gaps in even Fortune 100 companies between what Sales and

Marketing can produce, and what production or operations understand they need to deliver. Let's take them as they come.

Correct Standards

Do you want Paper or Plastic? Most standards aren't worth the paper they're printed on. Engineers develop them; not our Subject Matter Experts (SMEs). Why, because the SMEs haven't been trained on what or even why Standards are necessary or they don't have enough diplomas, or they can't be trusted not to set loose standards or worse yet --- that's not what we're paying them for.

In my opinion standards are usually arbitrarily set by managers or owners with little or no regard for input from the workforce, or even from customer requirement drivers for that matter. When (or if) our SMEs <u>are</u> included in the process, they are given standards for review, not to initiate or suggest changes.

Not long ago I was putting together a Best Method Practice program together for a Fortune 100 Company. When I went out on the floor to determine Standard Operating Procedures (SOPs) I asked experienced people on in the workplace what and how they were doing their tasks. Their reply shocked me.

"This is what is written up, but this is how we've figured out how to do it". When I asked them if they had informed Engineering of these deviations the reply was even more shocking: "Hell, they never ask us and we've given up trying to tell them." When I asked Engineering about it their reply was "Those people never talk to us, and besides, our SOPs come from corporate".

> *Δ People closest to the task*
> *know better how*
> *to do the task.*
>
> Tom Fehlman

We Are Standardized

There's enough here for a Waste Disposal Plant. Let's start with three groups of people doing the same tasks, or three operating shifts in the same department. I will show you a minimum of three various techniques used by the majority of people that have been taught by three separate trainers using <u>a minimum</u> of three various techniques over a period of time. That's a mouthful. But I'm not telling you what I think; I'm telling you what I know. There are four distinct levels of employee awareness at work here:

Unconsciously Incompetent When we have brand new people or people transferring to new jobs, they operate (or don't) at this level. At this stage they don't even know what they don't know. They are basically ignorant. We have all been at this level for various reasons, and we will all be there again at some point in time.

Consciously Incompetent People still can't do the job, but at this stage they are at least aware of what they don't know, usually because the boss has pointed out their ignorance to them. Incidentally, people at this stage are still usually cautious about the people and processes around them. The high Risk Takers come later.

Consciously Competent People can do the jobs with the speed, accuracy, efficiency and effectiveness of experienced people. They still have to think about what they're doing, but in the immortal words of Larry the Cable Guy, they can "get'er done!"

Unconsciously Competent In many respects our highest risks, because they are the most experienced. In manufacturing, this is where I find the most Medical or Lost Time Accidents. In the Service area, this is where I find the most "knacks" of dealing with customers that aren't documented.

And guess what, Sleepy Head? Who do we most often use to train our *Unconsciously Incompetent* people? You guessed it. **We use people that aren't thinking what they're doing to train people who have absolutely no idea what it is they are supposed to be doing.** (See "Sit by Nellie").

If we are going to standardize our processes and procedures, we must standard our application techniques, as well as standardize the ways and methods they are taught. Not doing so breeds unreliability and inconsistency by people who really want to do the job well. They've just never been really been given the chance to succeed from the first day on the job.

Δ Even If they Got It, It doesn't mean they Still Get It.

Tom Fehlman

We Are Seamless

Wake up and Smell It, and it's not Coffee. One operation I was recently in actually appeared "seamless" from Marketing through Scheduling. Unfortunately people making the stuff weren't in the loop. External Customers were actually provided fancy PERT charts and Critical Paths in order to track the flow of their orders.

However, Sales, Marketing, Scheduling and Manufacturing were all operating off of different schedules. Sales personnel were busy as usual getting as much business as they could, because that's how they are paid. Unfortunately, floor supervisors were not provided these fancy charts, basically because they were never trained to read them.

This appears to me to be Common Sense 101. Production personnel on the firing line were mad and frustrated as hell, because they were being asked questions by the Customer who was more informed than they were about their own work flow. Customers were actually coming out on the floor with their Critical Paths (provided by the Sales Department) and wondering why their product wasn't where it was supposed to be.

But for some reason senior management had not paid any attention to the madness and frustration of their own people. It's a "Catch 22" however, because PERT and Critical Path methodology that *Microsoft Projects©* and most other associated software programs generates, does not ensure accurate communication flow between the planners and doers. They simply point out where the most logical places to communicate are.

Look for programs that integrate the **scheduling of available resources together with the scheduling of tasks and activities.** Your next task is to ensure that **everyone speaks the same language at the same time.** We might actually have to look at how things work differently, and listen to people who are a lot closer to the problem.

> *Δ People need to be compensated for how the process works; not for how their silos work.*
>
> Tom Fehlman

Napkin Notes

- *Segments of the Process Need to be Tied together by Common "Payoffs" and Motivators.*
- *People Closest to the Process Need to be Involved in Its Construct*
- *Training in Processes Must be Standardized*
- *"Knacks" and Experience need to be Archived*
- *"Unconsciously Competent" Employees Must be Made Conscious*
- *Customers Should See Seamless*
- *Critical Paths should reflect Available Resources on a timeline as well as Tasks on a Timeline.*

Chapter 9: Lead, Follow or Change Your Pants

I heard this joke many years ago, and I have unashamedly used it frequently in many of my leadership workshops. It goes something like this:

> *During the American War for Independence a young American sea captain was sailing off the coast of North Carolina in his small frigate when a large British warship appeared over the horizon. The young captain turned to his even younger aide and said "Bring me my red coat!" The young aide quickly complied, the captain put the coat on; they fought the superior British and won the battle. The aide was impressed, but somewhat puzzled about the meaning of the red coat. He said nothing.*

> *Several days later, two large British warships appeared on the horizon, the young captain again requested his red coat which was quickly provided by his aide, and the Americans again won against overwhelming odds. The aide was not only impressed, but now was driven to find out about the apparent magic of the red coat. He asked his captain to explain. "This is a valuable lesson for you", replied the young captain. "You are the model for your men. They must never see you hurt, wounded or waver. The red coat covers up any injuries I may receive during battle."*

> *This explanation made a lot of sense to the young aide, and the journey continued. Three days later an entire British fleet appeared over the horizon, and the captain cried out "**Bring me my brown pants!**"*

Now you see why some of my workshop participants have actually voted to limit the number of jokes I'm allowed to tell. However, the joke does raise an interesting point on when to lead and when to follow. Even more interesting to me is the issue of when to fight and when to retreat. Should we only fight the battles we are sure of winning?

In union settings, I have encountered many grizzled supervisors who have given up on implementing corrective action, or maintaining discipline. Their rationale is disturbing, but hard to argue with. The point they make is "I used to write people up when they got out of line. But the union would always grieve, and somewhere in a back room my discipline got traded away by upper management as a concession to the union in order to achieve some kind of higher management objective.

So why go through the hassle of writing people up, when it just get traded away? It's a lot easier to look the other way." To compound the problem, they are often told by the union, and not their own management, that they "lost the battle". There are times when ethically and morally you must fight tactical battles you are destined to lose, in order to strategically win the hearts and minds of the people who have chosen to follow you.

"Falling on Your Sword" is unfortunately out of fashion. Upper mobility and compliance has taken the place of the ethical leadership of people. Fighting the implementation of a major change program when your people are not mentally ready to absorb it is a great example of the point I'm making.

Middle and lower levels of leadership constantly "roll over" when they're charged by those above with implementing a major change program to take place "next Monday". Simply moving people from one desk to another initiates a change cycle that people need a little time to adjust to. If we don't protect our people, who will? Even if it means changing our pants, some things are worth putting our professional lives on the line for.

In simple terms it breaks down to (1) **Lead** when you must, (2) **Follow** when you can, and (3) **Get Back Jack** when you are serving no purpose in the first two positions. If you are *Leading* when you have to, *Following* when others are more suited to lead, you will create a healthy environment in which you are not necessary for routine, daily activity. Getting "out of the way" is a position that good leaders aspire to. The true irony is that the more effort you put into proving how valuable you are to the organization, the more expendable you actually become.

Δ *Good leadership may mean an occasional change of your pants*

Tom Fehlman

Driving Tasks/Steering People

Recently I had the opportunity to assess the leadership capabilities of a former US Air Force Academy graduate. His job was to provide field customer service, working with field technicians. The field technicians I'm talking about here are comprised mainly of hard working, hard playing, no-nonsense type of technicians. The majority, were male, and had no problems settling labor disputes out in the parking lot. They often used concise, four-letter words in describing issues, events and people (My kind of people).

Without any background knowledge, the young man was amazed that within 5 minutes of the assessment I identified him as a "Zoomie", or former Air Force cadet. I explained to him that when I saw someone with an F-18 fighter jet stuck up his butt, it was fairly easy to figure out where his head was.

If you looked up the definition of rigid and structured in the dictionary, you would find a picture of this guy in full dress uniform. He was argumentative for no other reason than the need to be right. He denied making statements that both I and my fellow assessor had captured in direct quotes.

When asked to engage in free-form discussions, he stated he was much more comfortable in describing his "process". He used precise language and clipped words such as "sir" and "understood" in response to our coaching. This guy made George Patton look like Pee Wee Herman.

Our young friend was much more interested in "winning the battle" than learning from his mistakes. His need to "be right" and "look good; smell good" defined his personal ethics. He finally understood what the intent of a developmental leadership assessment was only when we used "shock and awe" feedback with him. A recent follow up with his manager indicates that he is slowly learning through the accumulation of "scar tissue"; which is not the recommended way to learn when you have other resources available.

Do It or Die

One of the more intriguing arguments our Academy friend used on us was that once people got to know him, after five or six weeks, he began to loosen up and people began to trust him. My succinct rebuttal to him was that he wouldn't live long enough for people to begin to trust him. Most folks I know would begin a "scorched earth" strategy on him before his first day ended.

Subordinates don't have to like you, but they better be able to tolerate you, or your career will suffer a quick and painful death. Control of the workplace and caring about your people are not mutually exclusive. Control Freaks "freak" out people who work for them.

Why not take those personal attributes that eventually cause people to trust and relate to us, and use them in the beginnings of relationships rather than toward the end of relationships. Being rigid and structured gives people the impression that we are distant, aloof and not caring. There are times when you must be rigid and structured, but they should fit the situation, and not just our own personal comfort zone.

Good leaders learn to follow. Good leaders coach people because they care about them. Are we doing things for our sake, or for our peoples' benefit? Allowing our people at times to see our human side is not a bad thing. Admitting our mistakes to subordinates who already know we made them, even if we have to "Change our Pants" to do it, is an important ingredient of holistic leadership.

Napkin Notes

- *Leadership is Risky Business*
- *Look for opportunities to show Vulnerability*
- *You Can't Coach People if You Don't Care About Them*
- *If You don't Trust Them; They Won't Trust You*
- *You May Have to Lose Battles to Win Wars*
- *If You Don't Protect Your People, Who Will?*
- *When You're on the Leadership Train, you only Have Three Options*

Chapter 10: People Are Our Most Valuable Assets

This twisted take on reality really stinks up the place. I was once charged with doing an Outplacement Program while management decided to put down new carpet in the hallways. That certainly managed a good impression as people being let go walked around carpet installers. Back in my formative years I was actually told by a mentor "Get your people to buy a new trailer or car, so they got to come to work".

Talk about Mixed Messages! And I have seen glaring evidence of these bald-faced lies every day since in both the public and private sectors. We put people in leadership positions for management reasons, and put people in management positions for leadership reasons. We ride our good horses hard and put them "up wet". We have different standards for our people who "Walk on Water", as opposed to our "Seeds of Satan".

We hold people accountable when they shouldn't be, and we don't hold people accountable when they should be. And every day *we walk past people doing good work without even noticing it*. Surely "goodness and mercy" <u>will not follow</u> people who are not screwing up enough to get noticed.

My Job Is to Find Problems

Give me some dinosaur repellant! This position lost its credibility somewhere around the Cro Magnum period. However, the old adage "Manage from the left and Lead from the right" certainly applies here. For instance, why would people other than marginal performers support a union campaign? Because what they're doing apparently doesn't matter to anyone.

When I ask groups, "how many people here have put written commendations in peoples' files as opposed to written reprimands?" I consistently find about **2 to 1** in favor of written reprimands. The next question obviously is "are we subconsciously creating negative or positive work climates for our people to function in?"

The answer is a resounding Hell No! We won't change cultures until we change attitudes and related behaviors. The problem is, without some type of prompt or accountability, regardless of our awareness the "Tyranny of the Urgent Task" kicks in as soon as we feel some pressure to perform.

We forget the simple principle that we are only as good as we allow our people to be. Remember, we need to look for **4** things people are doing correctly for every **1** thing we find them lacking in. Leadership is a balance between task and relationships. Your position in that balance is dictated by the situation, not by your comfort zone.

> *Δ Remember the 4 to 1*
> *Law. Four Positives to*
> *Every Negative!*
>
> Tom Fehlman

Consistency is the Key

Another laugher! This myth has been around forever and a day. Let's talk reality here. I enthusiastically embrace the notion that that are standards of performance that must be adhered to. However, people must be led differently to those standards. What have I found in over 7000 leadership assessments? Far too many "wanna be" leaders believe that consistency means style. They use Policy as Absolutes.

If you want black and white Absolutes, get a union and manage a contract. The pre-requisite for this type of manger is being able to read. Leadership works best in the "gray" areas. Let's assume I have ten people working for me. For consistency and argument's sake let's assume they all make $20 an hour.

Two can **Walk on Water.** For every messy, critical situation that comes up, these folks will get it done. They are basically on call; day, night or even while on vacation. They give me about 120% day in and day out.

At least while their internal combustion mechanism is up and working, since they don't get "fueled up" much from outside resources. They don't like to be micro managed, so I am careful not to give them any attention whatsoever unless it's an emergency.

Six of my people are **Swimmers.** These are good people; the backbone of my little group. They are usually not going to set any speed records, but at least they're in the water and getting wet. They give me about 90 to 95% on a regular basis. Work couldn't get done without them.

Ironically, these folks who are my biggest opportunity for overall improvement get the least amount of attention of my three groups. Seldom do they do more than is required. Seldom do they do enough to really get me "peed off". They are, after all, Average. My time is better spent doing, oh, whatever.

Two of my people are the **Treaders.** They are my *Seeds of Satan*, and I'm convinced the only reason they exist is to make my management life on earth a living Hell. They will give me 50 to 60% on a good day, with the right alignment of the moon and stars. Not only do they take up a lot of my own valuable time, but the rest of my people must make up what they miss.

It is a classic Pareto pattern, in that 80% of my time is spent micromanaging people who are going to be responsible for at minimum 2% of whatever success my group achieves. It's a really damn good thing I got good people who do what they do for reasons I have yet to fathom.

And I got balloons big enough to say I'm Consistent. The team met its goals, so I am going to give everyone a Chicken Dinner. I heard somewhere in a workshop far, far away in another galaxy that it's good to reinforce good behavior and celebrate success. Since I'm too busy to track individual progress and contributions, my only option is to reinforce the entire team.

My **Walk on Waters** (who got badly burned wings, incidentally) are sitting next to my **Seeds** who are savoring their thighs and breasts. I wonder what's going through their minds. I bet you know, if you stop right now and think about it. My good guys are wondering what they're busting their butts for. My Satanists are thinking "Hey, this isn't a bad gig".

Of course, my **Swimmers** stay as confused as ever. What does Good look like, anyway? And what's the Payoff? And who was Pareto anyway? Whoever he was, he knew a bunch about the distribution of chicken dinners.

Δ Be Consistent with Standards, not how you lead people to them.

Tom Fehlman

My People Know What To Expect

Let me cash your reality check here. Every day your people expect something between Dr. Jekyll and Mr. Hyde to show up in the morning. A supervisor nicknamed Sparky once told me, "I treat my people all the same, and they all think I'm an SOB". In a weird, twisted way there is something to be said for that, although not a lot of good can be said for that.

Today when the pressure of the task is off I will give you credit for checking in with your people, asking how the families are (but we don't want to get too personal now, do we?), and chatting a little about the latest reality show or last minute field goal. Tomorrow when the *pressure is on* I'll bet you will either consciously or unconsciously walk past the same people without giving them the time of day.

You don't mean to do it, but you have no idea what type of ripple effect you just caused. People will be thinking everything from the "boss is really pissed off" to "I wonder what I've done wrong". And since they never get a chance to give you feedback on your behavior, you will continue to think in your blissful ignorance that you are a consistent leader, and that your people love and respect you. Have another cup of our special lemonade.

Δ Coaches demonstrate caring on a consistent basis

Tom Fehlman

HIPPA Is A Bunch of HYPA

I understand and support the need for privacy, but I don't want you playing with my subordinates with your strict rules and policies. We haven't taken the time to train our management teams on when it applies, and when it doesn't. This is some of that Politically Correct non-sense I mentioned earlier.

I'm sure some of my industry colleagues (notice I didn't say friends) will disagree with me on this issue. My viewpoint is that the Privacy Act and associated new policies and procedures, if interpreted incorrectly, pose one of the biggest potential threats to trust and relationship building between leaders and subordinates that I have seen yet.

People continually tell me they don't want to "pry" into subordinate lives. Some newer managers have told me they are even afraid to recognize pain by saying phrases such as "I'm sorry you're going through some problems". I don't want them to pry; but I do <u>want them to probe.</u> The more data you get, the better informed decision you can make on a personal leadership level.

Policies are often used as absolutes primarily because they are misunderstood in their application. Very seldom have I found senior management and/or human resources taking the time to really explain the intent of these policies to their immediate first line leadership.

When I conduct Assessment Centers, I find an appalling number of first and second tier leaders that do not have a basic grasp on fundamental policy and procedure that apply directly to them.

Δ Don't Ask-Don't Tell- means nobody learns anything from anyone.

Tom Fehlman

I am told every day by misguided managers that they can no longer ask a subordinate what's wrong, or is there a problem you want to talk about, or what's getting in the way? When we reach the point where all the do-gooders prohibit our leadership from determining cause and effect of personnel problems, sign over the title of the asylum to the inmates and let them run it.

When the boss can't say "I'm sorry you're going through that" because he/she is not allowed to hear what's going on, as leaders we are quite literally "dead in the water". If my wife is sick, I might actually appreciate my leader providing me some verbal support- if I so choose. *Bonding, commitment and loyalty* occur because of known concern and caring the leader has for his/her subordinates.

Of course leaders have the right to ask about personal issues that are creating professional problems. Just as employees have the right not to answer those questions. If we lose the right to demonstrate care and concern about our people and their families, we have lost the ability motivate, reinforce and coach.

> *Δ People don't leave their personal problems outside the gate. We don't, and they don't.*
>
> Tom Fehlman

Napkin Notes

- *Lead People Differently to Consistent Standards*
- *You Have the right to Ask; They Have the Right Not to Answer*
- *People don't Leave Their Problems "Outside the Gate".*
- *Look for and Respond to Peoples' Pain*
- *Loyalty, Commitment and Sacrifice Come from Caring*
- *Take the time to train the Letter and Intent of Laws, Policies and Procedures*
- *Remember the 4 to 1 Law. Four Positives for Every Negative*

Chapter 11: Minds Over Matters

To get their minds right, you got to get their hearts right. Every employee contains two separate people. Every person who has a position has some level of pain or some type of emotional investment in that position. Where there is a behavioral problem, there is some type of emotional payoff that causes that behavior to exist.

Anger is a symptom of Pain. Frustration is a symptom of Pain. Resisting Change is a symptom of Pain. You get the idea. Effective leadership deals in balance between problems and pain. I don't want to hear about your noble, task-driven **BS (Belief Systems)** when I got my own pain. If you consider yourself a leader, you must consider yourself a *Behaviorist*. How many of us understand behavior, or have studied techniques of behavior modification? You consider yourself a problem solver; stick to the tangibles.

There is a story I like to tell about Hannibal crossing the desert with his army. The army began to run short of water, and scouts were urgently sent out to find new water sources. They can back finding only half a jug full of water, which they immediately took to the great general so at least he could drink.

Hannibal called his entire army together, and in front of his massed troops poured the half jug of water on the ground. He is reported to have said "It does no good for one to drink when so many thirst". Unless you've had all your nerve endings removed, that should send shivers up your spine.

No doubt in my mind that his troops would follow him through hell band back at that point. There was not rant about "buckle up" or "grin and bear it". He never even mentioned the mission. Hannibal understood that acknowledging the pain of others bought him loyalty he could buy from no other source.

*Δ **To get their hearts right,
you got to get their hearts' rate.***

Tom Fehlman

Deteriorated Children

One of the first things to understand about adult behavior is that we are all simply ***deteriorated children***. Understand it, and accept it. Our motives may be somewhat more complex, primarily because as adults we have to deal with more scar tissue than kids do. However, once the public school system gets ahold of the little people, and knocks what little creativity out of us that we had as children, we're basically all about the same.

Our drivers are different, but our feelings are much the same. As adults, we still get angry, jealous, fearful, or silly. We're still reactionary, we still get our feelings hurt, we still seek power as protection, and I still like to be right, which may mean making you wrong. **We still know what's going to play when we "push each others' buttons"**

Don't ask what's wrong with people. Remember, they're asking the same questions about you. Dig below what you see or hear, to find the stimulators and motivators. Drive to the **Drivers**. All behavior comes from either Antecedents (instinct, promises, conditioning, etc.) or Consequences (payoffs, rewards, etc.) You control behavior only to what *Span of Control* you have over either or both. If you don't control primary Antecedents or Consequences, there's not a damn thing you can do about behavior.

Δ Adults are simply deteriorated children.

Tom Fehlman

Symptoms vs Causes

Good leaders do not treat Symptoms as **Causes**. Unfortunately as leaders, the first things we notice or that hits us between the eyes, are the symptoms of problems. Let's say Johnny didn't show up for work today. As you work through your initial "pissed offedness" you debate on whether or not to write bad Johnny up. He's spoiled your day, and now you got to cover his work.

And, best of all, your handy dandy policy or union contract grants you permission to write him up. Believe it or not, you got some choices here. You can administer your policy or procedure. Or you can choose the more difficult leadership route, which means determining the cause before you take action.

Absenteeism is a symptom of a cause. Sure, you can apply policy or a contract to address the symptom of absenteeism. That's easy, and calls for little more than the ability to read. There are certainly times when the behavior is so egregious, or the performance so unfixable, you need to apply policy.

Johnny may well be a "Seed of Satan", and if he is I'll use policy quicker than anyone to show him the door. But if he's salvageable, and I still have some time to work with, I will attempt to work on the cause. That means listening with empathy, and coaching with caring.

Δ Applying policy solves symptoms; not causes.

Tom Fehlman

Napkin Notes

- *Generals Relate to the Common Soldiers' Pain*
- *Policy Addresses Symptoms; Leadership Drives to Causes*
- *All Behavior Comes from Antecedents and/or Consequences*
- *Listen and Respond with Empathy*
- *Don't Apply Your BS (Belief Systems) to Your employees*
- *Know Your Behavioral Span of Control*
- *Adults are Simply Deteriorated Children.*

Chapter 12: The Buck Stops Here

Brother, can you spare a dime? When is the last time you heard a manager posing as a leader say "Gang, I'm sorry; I screwed up!" Of course, if that happens too often that manager/leader will soon be selling used cars for a living. However, I've heard it so infrequently I actually find it refreshing.

The fact of the matter is, when we mess up as leaders the people most affected by the mistake already know who, why, and what happened. In the old cotton mill days, we used to call this type of smokescreen the "Waterhouse Rumor". If you wanted the truth, go to the waterhouse. (a textile restroom to the uninformed).

The waterhouse usually contained true and accurate information that management was afraid to tell us. The amazing thing is as a supervisor I often relied on my subordinates to know what was going on, and went to the waterhouse frequently for things other than viewing nature up front.

That is because as a supervisor we were not viewed or trusted as management by management. If the rumors weren't true, more often than not they were worse than the truth turned out to be, and had an even more negative impact on peoples' performance and attitudes.

We don't need a sign on the desk saying the "Buck Stops Here." With all due respect, Mr. Truman, our people already got that not so subtle message from the organizational chart. As Leaders, if we cover and run, We are fooling only ourselves, in hopes of retaining whatever credibility and respect we may have acquired up to that point in time.

Remember, leadership is risky business. If you do it right you're going to take hits, sometimes by Friendly Fire. Ironically, admitting to errors in judgment or performance (in moderation, of course) does not increase our interpersonal risk, but rather reduces our interpersonal risk. Honesty is not only the Best Policy; it is the <u>Only Option</u> when we deal with subordinates, peers, customers or others. Of course you may have to lie like a sleeping dog to the boss to CYA, but that's expected. (Just kidding to see if you're paying attention).

They Can't Be Trusted With the Information

And management can, I guess! And exactly why it that? It must have something to do with the organizational chart, or educational level, or intelligence quotients, or salary, or power, or personal charm, or the fact that they drink beer and you drink whiskey sours. Now I am not naïve to the point that I believe all information all the time is open for distribution.

But I do believe that most people can be trusted most of the time. In today's organization, information is like currency, or the air we breathe. Limit the input, and people begin to choke on ignorance and uncertainty. In the Air Force, as an officer in the Strategic Air Command, I had a Top Secret Crypto Clearance, which meant I had access to the "Go Codes" or Launch Codes.

I knew where the nuclear payloads were headed, what orphanages in China and Russia had been targeted, and obviously access was limited. However, even raw rookie airmen could figure out the general direction things were headed. Everyone knew who the common potential enemy was, and why some data was limited and some wasn't. I don't have a big problem with people not being told things, compared to a major heartburn in people not knowing **why** they aren't being told things.

Δ If you don't trust your people, they won't trust you

Tom Fehlman

74

They Are Not Capable of Understanding

I probably wouldn't have noticed this one, until my twelve year old granddaughter told me I wasn't capable of understanding some of the new music she likes to hear. I told her in a very polite way that I knew enough about it not to like it, at which point she told me something I can't repeat in this book.

Because many in our workforce work on very specialized, tactical things, it doesn't mean they can't understand, or more importantly won't work to understand, sophisticated, strategic issues that affect them long term. In military elite teams such as the Seals, Berets, and Recon, everyone on the team is briefed on tactical issues that in fact could have strategic national security repercussions, regardless of their rank or tenure on the team.

> *Δ Many employees are smart enough to turn down management positions*
>
> Tom Fehlman

It Doesn't Apply to Them

Or "they won't be interested". I actually agree with this myth in terms of how information is actually presented to people, although I strongly disagree with the reasons for it. Most of the verbiage that comes out of the rarefied air of boardrooms is fit only for accountants to read, because it's in a different language for the rest of mankind to read.

It's no surprise that many "Communication Specialists" hired by large corporations don't get it, because they've never been exposed to the different languages spoken in organizations. These languages are vastly different one from another, because each is tied to the reality of the position and the specific tasks involved. Basically the Language Pyramid works like this:

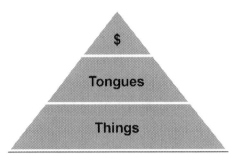

A. The **Language of Money**. This is a language almost exclusively used by upper management, and ties directly to EBIT, Costs, Variables, Overhead, Sales, and basic Profit and Loss. It's the language they talk in, and the language they use to talk to others in. Frankly, Scarlett, I don't really give a damn if our profit is 1.5M or 1.8M, and as far as I know I've never met one of these stockholders you're always talking about. I'm much more concerned as a toolgrinder that if what you're talking about means, I got a job next month that sure does apply to me.

B. The **Language of Tongues**. This is where middle to lower supervision falls. Folks caught here or literally "caught in the middle" when it comes to language barriers. They must become experts in speaking "in tongues". They must interpret money language coming down on them from high, as well as interpreting "thing" language coming at them from lower levels of the organization.

C. The **Language of Things.** Here I am again, your friendly, inquisitive toolgrinder. I'm talking in the "Thing" language, which includes who's here and who isn't, what job is next to complete, and why my supervisor has this questioning look on his face as he attempts to tell me what direction top management is taking the company in. And what's this mission statement got to do with me. Incidently, I got no customers, cause I never see 'em and never talk to them.

As a Behavior Manager, I would sometimes watch people walk past the company bulletin board coming to work. Next to the company bulletin board was the Board of Interest, where folks could post their boat for sale, or look for a ride to Florida. Almost everyone walked past the company board without even so much as a glance, because it was written in "management" language, and didn't apply to the state of their particular nation.

Gradually, management learned that if there was an important news flash that people needed information on, don't post it on the company board with the rules, regulations and federal laws. Put it on the Board of Interest, and hold a workplace meeting on the topic to ensure both *Visually* and *Verbally* oriented employees got the message.

Supervisors get upset because they feel upper management doesn't listen or care about their problems. Workforces get upset because they aren't "being heard" by upper management. Upper management makes arbitrary decisions on what applies, and what doesn't. Doesn't anyone out there hear me? You are communicating in the wrong language. Let me decide if it applies to me, if I understand what you're talking about.

Δ *Talk is Cheap, regardless of the language.*

Tom Fehlman

Chapter 13: Caught In The Headlights

This title implies exactly what I mean by it. From the outside looking in, leadership can appear to be fairly simple. Many "wannabe" managers who attend my assessment center end up surprised and even shocked that Leadership is sometimes more behavior based than task focused. Anoint some managers with the holy water of the implied power of Leadership and get ready for sermons, unilateral decisions, lectures and monologues.

And it seems that the higher up the intellectual scale they go, the wider their eyes get. Whatever happened to common sense, instinct and intuition? Talk to me about the common sense of senior management when I'm conducting outplacement services for long-time employees while new, expensive carpet is being put down in the hallway outside my office.

Tell me about the long term plant manager from a government agency who finds out he's being terminated from friends a week before he's officially notified by his management because they're afraid to confront him. Explain to me how a large international company could actually build a factory before they had figured out how to build the product. Tell me about the candidates for management that I assessed as being "Not Ready"; who were promoted in spite of my predictions and had union campaigns underway at their locations within a year.

For some reason arrogance and self assuredness takes precedent over actually having skills. They were promoted not because they could handle the job. They were promoted because their management had led them to believe that within a certain time frame, if they achieved a certain level of task results they would be promoted. How many promotions involve criteria such as *firm but fair* or *a caring coach?* These **accidental promotions** happen (and continue) in organizations that everyone would recognize. Carrying a Day Timer™ does not a leader make.

Since I Told You, You Should Get It

The ability to delude yourself is an important survival tool. This is basic Communication Skills 101. And throw in a little delegation skills for good measure. If you're the boss, and you tell an employee to do something important, there may be a myriad of reasons he/she will say "yes sir/yes ma'am" to you, and walk off muttering to themselves "damifino".

The employee may have too much pride to admit ignorance, or hope they can figure out the assignment as it goes along. They may even be afraid of disappointing you, the boss. I have already mentioned I also get a kick out of companies and managers who post important notices on the Employee Bulletin board, and then sit back and wonder why nobody is reading such an important announcement.

Well, some are but many are not. The same holds true, and even more so, of emails, or "ebombs" as some folks call them. If you want a really fun time, ask some employees what the company Mission Statement is. I'll even let you let them stand under the sign as you ask them. When they look at you like you're a side dish they didn't order, don't be surprised. Just look at the Language!

The fact is, we communicate with each other in different channels, at different levels. The problem is that you and I will communicate in the channel we are most comfortable using in sending it out, not necessarily the channel other people are using to receive it. In my experience, people tend to be:

Visual Don't call me or tell me the message. Give it to me to read, or paint me a picture. I need time to analyze and absorb what you need to communicate to me. We can talk about it later if we have to.

Verbal I've got to wade through thirty emails already today. If it's important, tell me face to face or over the phone. If you feel better, send me an email as a reminder.

Experiential How would you communicate to someone about how much pressure to put on a brake to slow down a car? Telling them wouldn't get it completely, and giving them a paragraph to read won't get the job done either. People also communicate through the sense of touch, feel, taste and smell. Let me experience it or sense it; then I will understand the importance of it.

The more important the message, the more channels we should use in communicating it. Post it, have workplace meetings, and allow people to participate in the implementation. Otherwise, don't blame the guy behind the tree for not doing it. If you haven't used all the normal channels of communication open to you, guess what? Tag, You're It.

Δ Orders go down; Reality goes up!

Author Unknown

We Have an Open Door Policy

Probably because some irate employee stole the door!! I must confess at one time I was guilty of teaching the "criticize in private; praise in public" axiom. The first part about "criticizing in private" is still spot on, but the second part is by necessity negotiable. I first heard this gem of using public praise from some guy in the "Ivory Tower" teaching me Behavior Management thirty years ago.

Funny how some of this theory didn't work well on the second shift with two people missing, and all hell breaking loose, but it worked well under controlled environments with mice, rats and several types of "managers". However, I've now seen and heard enough managers and supervisors complaining over the years that nobody ever comes to see them in their office unless it's a complaint or a problem.

Big surprise! Nothing good or positive ever happens in the office. The problem is easily solved. Find a <u>neutral setting</u> for discussions concerning individual performance or behavior. Use the office to issue written commendations as well as written warnings. Remember back in the day when students got called to the vice principal's office in high school.

That's where they kept the body bags. And they made it worse by announcing over the PA system that you were to report to the VP's office. (Thank goodness that never happened to me!).I don't remember anyone ever dropping in there to have a friendly chit-chat with the V.P.

Δ *If you want to housebreak a dog; don't expect the dog to fetch the paper for you*

Tom Fehlman

I've also seen employees extremely embarrassed by public displays of praise. I once put up the picture and performance chart of an employee who was truly excelling at his job. Unfortunately, I didn't see the need to check with him beforehand to see how he felt about such a display in front of his peers.

I was guilty of placing my own values and BS (Belief Systems) on his motivation. The next morning both the chart and the picture made a nice pile of chaff. Who was the perpetrator of this dastardly deed? No, it wasn't the other employees, but it certainly could have been.

It was the employee I was attempting to honor and motivate. It seemed like a good idea to me at the time. And even the damn book I was reading on Behavior Modification, written as it turns out by theorists; recommended the technique. I ended up embarrassing the poor guy, and he never forgot; nor did his peers allow him to forget.

I'd like to take all these "Ivory Tower" PhD theorists and transport them to a deserted island, and let them theorize how to get off. Things work differently in the real world at 2:00 a.m. on a swing shift in a manufacturing plant than they do in a clinic.

> *Δ Rewards should be meaningful to the people who get them; not necessarily to the people that give them.*
>
> Tom Fehlman

I'll Listen to What You Have to Say

This one is hard to write, let alone say with a straight face. What a bunch of poppycaca. You are much more interested in giving information than getting it. The vast majority and I do mean vast; of leadership assessment simulations I've given over the past twenty years end up with the boss doing 80% of the talking throughout their simulations.

They made the mistake of actually listening to someone who at one time told them that they were the Boss, and therefore must tell people what to do. This is almost the mirror opposite of what should be happening. 60% of a leader's time should be taken up in listening, around 30% in talking, and 10% in purely observing. Listening is not a lost art. When did we ever have it?

It's amazing to me that very few school systems include Active Listening skills in any of their curricula, at any level. And we wonder why people grow up to be non listeners. When I give pre and post tests in my Effective Listening program, I often see increases of up to 75% effectiveness in listening skills.

People are amazed to discover that listening in large part is an operant or a learned skill. It's hard work. And it can be physically exhausting if it's done right. But I wonder how many of you reading this book right now have ever attended a listening skills workshop. After all, it's one of the "soft skills", isn't it? And when you have a lot of "tasks" to do, who the hell needs soft skills? Listening, possibly the most important of all leadership skills is one that comes to us freely, if we just listen for it.

Δ *Listening is the absence of Talking.*

Author Unknown

I'm Committed, Why Aren't You

"Committed" is the operative word here. People don't show up to work **committed**. If you believe that, you need to be "committed". We are talking about that old transfer of values and BS (belief systems-Got YA!) When you want me to give you something like commitment, you'd better give me something in return. And it better be meaningful, or

I'll give you conformity, but not commitment. If you want to be an upward mobile workaholic and spend 60 hours at work, I'm happy for you. You may go far down the road to increased responsibility. But don't transfer your crap to me. I already got enough of my own to deal with.

I may have kids to take to ballgames, or a poker club at my house this week. I may actually enjoy what I do outside of work, even in moderation. Your professional tasks do not automatically become my personal goals.

Your priorities are probably not mine. Of course, you could ask me what mine are and we could work together toward what the high priced consultants call "mutual objectives". But if you insist on being the "boss" --- I'll let you. Until I find a place and people, where my needs get some damn attention. Remember, your problem is not with the people that leave. It's with the people you keep.

I had an interesting experience just the other night. I went to my favorite watering hole for a little "Pain Go Bye-Bye" juice and some trivia. It was also "All you Can Eat" Crableg night. What happened can only be termed as commonly bizarre. While the boss was out schmoozing with the clientele, unbeknownst to him the cook had worked out a deal with the dishwasher to cover his cooking job for him.

The Crablegs came out very clean but barely edible. My guess is that somebody is gonna pay. And, besides his lost business, it won't be the manager. I will also project that the cook was never told by the manager he could not delegate his cooking responsibilities to the dishwasher.

Our value system tells us that common sense dictates the answer. Unfortunately this value system may not be shared with everyone coming from Guadalajara, or Alabama, or wherever. It's a shame. The cook and the dishwasher were pretty good at doing their designated jobs. Wonder who isn't?

> *Δ We lose our good people;*
> *not the ones we are*
> *supposed to get rid of.*
>
> Tom Fehlman

Call Me "Mr. Motivation"

Excuse me while my Gag Reflex kicks in. Where are we hiding all these great Visionary Leaders and Sublime Motivators? Your job isn't to motivate anybody! Your job is to create an environment in which people can become motivated. Many years ago now a well-meaning Maintenance Manager I worked with wanted to "reinforce" his mechanics by taking them to the best steak restaurant in town; to reward them for a "job well done".

You know the kind of place I'm talking about. Big steaks and ridiculously small salad bowls. Knuckle-headed me actually approved the plan. I decided to tag along to ensure everything went smoothly, and I liked the bar (and barmaids) at this place. Of course everything went predictably "un-smoothly".

Would you have guessed that the Maintenance Manager liked steak? Naturally. Would you guess that the majority of these mechanics liked steak? No brainer. Would you have guessed that several of the mechanics were actually vegetarians? Hardly. After talking to them after the meal,

I was amazed to find out that they were actually de-motivated by the experience of sitting next to people eating animals.

Imagine that. Not all people are motivated by the same things. Keep your Motivators to yourself. Find out what makes me run hard, and give me a chance to get it with as much frequency as possible.

Let's take a group of ten or more people. I can consistently predict that somewhere in the neighborhood that, 75% of them when given the chance to immediately choose a number between 1 and 4, will for some reason choose <u>3</u>. How do I know this? Because Leaders lead Behavior, and I've studied behavior firsthand! I can't tell you why 3 is so predictable, but that really isn't the issue, is it? Most behavior is predictable most of the time in most controlled environments. Left to its own devices, behavior will go pretty damn much where it wants to. Have you or the so-called leaders around you studied behavior techniques or modification? Ah, Ha, I suspected as much. Become a Master of Modification, and you can become a Master of Motivation.

Δ Don't talk to me about bulls unless you've learned about them in the bullring.

Author Unknown

Napkin Notes

- *Use balanced task and behavioral criteria in selecting managers*
- *Verbal, Visual and Experiential Communication Should be Geared to the Receiver, not the Sender.*
- *Conformity is Not Commitment*
- *Orders go Down; Reality Goes Up.*
- *Use Your Office for Positive as Well as Negative Discussions*
- *The Ability to Listen is the most under-rated and under-utilized Leadership skill.*
- *Delegation Needs to Specifically Define the boundaries of Ownership*
- *Don't transfer your Personal B.S. (Belief Systems) to your employees*
- *Mastering the Techniques of Motivation is Based on Mastering Behavior Management*

Chapter 14: Colorless, Odorless, Tasteless

Let's talk about Passion, which at my age most often comes in the form of fruit. If a doctor is trying to cure me of the many different types of crap running through my body; I don't want him to probe me in <u>moderation</u>; I want him to probe me in <u>excess</u>. (I realize I may live long enough to regret that statement.)

Work on me passionately, brother or sister doctor. Use all your knowledge, and do it enthusiastically! I understand there is risk involved, but I suspect it's even riskier for me long term if you don't. Good doctors have a lot in common with good leaders.

Leadership is risky business. If you have the personality and energy of tofu, I don't want you leading the troops. They need more color, flavor and taste from you. Situational Leadership is just that. You got to be able to read the tea leaves, and adjust.

You may not have all the data you're comfortable with, but sometimes your gut has to lead your head. And get used to the idea of playing a large number of different roles, whether you are comfortable with them or not.

(**SEE Role Path**).

»»»»»»»»»»»»»»»»»»»»»»»»»

A. Vlad the Impaler *Conform or die!*
B. Patton *Binary Thinking in terms of Right vs. Wrong*
C. Martin Luther King *Inspired Leadership*
D. Gandhi *Visionary Leadership*
E. Mother Teresa *Role Model*
F. Teddy Bear *Friend to All*

Vlad the Impaler

I lead; You follow. There are high consequences for non conformity. You exist at my pleasure. Live by the Sword and Die by the Sword. Control is everything.

George Patton

He/She has High concern for task, which makes him/her admired by those who survive the task. High risk taker because of political insensitivity.

Occasional delusions of grandeur. High in aggression, low in tolerance.

Martin Luther King

Impassioned and spiritual Leadership. Impatient with small steps. Extroverted and Strategically flexible. Sensitive to public opinion and manipulation of communication. Part authoritarian and part lassiez-faire. Knows how to play both sides against the middle.

Mahatma Gandhi

Introverted and Internally driven. Most comfortable with indirect confrontation. Takes tactical hits to achieve long term goals. Patient and tolerant. Assertive but not aggressive. Often uses humor to convey strong thoughts or feelings.

Mother Teresa

People and relationships more important than task. Models strength and commitment by example. Non confrontational. Driven by internal standards. Personal sacrifice irrelevant, as long as others' needs are met.

Teddy Bear

Likes to be liked. More comfortable with Coaching than Leading. Gets along to get along. Has many desires, but few requirements that call for total commitment. Easily delegates both Authority and Responsibility.

There are times you have to play Patton, and times you have to play Gandhi, and you have to be believable in both roles to win the Leadership Oscar. What happens if the boss tells you your people have to work New Years Eve in order to get the project done? You know there will be resistance, and you yourself don't even see the need for such an extreme move. But the boss is adamant.

You must be able to sell your people on the idea, overcome anticipated resistance from some of your "Seeds" and if necessary draw a clear line in the sand about what must be done. You've got to play three roles in the same meeting! Start with Gandhi (or Mother Teresa if you prefer); evolve through Martin Luther King and elevate if you must to Patton.

You must be able to go from supporting and nurturing to the classic "hard ass", and be convincing in both. Tofu Leadership won't get it because it is not capable of doing it. It is impractical, if not impossible, to be a 'vanilla-flavored" leader the majority of time. Practice in front of the mirror.

If you're the leader, coach and role play with your folks before sending them into battle. Better yet, go to your local Toastmasters and get needed feedback. Buy the Situational Leadership book by Dr. Paul Hersey. If you are animated and passionate with your kids or significant other, take some of it to work with you.

That's Just the Way I Am

If you buy into this, I'd like to rub your nose in it. The classic of copouts. "I'm always late to meetings; that's just the way I am". We are the way we choose to be. Change is work and Change is risky and often Change is not comfortable. When we have to slam on the brakes because Richard Petty just pulled out suddenly in front of us; that makes us angry.

When we didn't get that promotion we thought we had bagged, that makes us sad or depressed. When that subordinate does not do it the way we wanted him/her to, that makes us upset and frustrated. When our "Significant Other" forgot to take the garbage out, that really steams our clams.

"I'm not Reactive, and I hate it when people say I am". If it doesn't make sense, and it's not appropriate for the situation; choose not to be that way. You can't make me feel anything I don't want to feel, or that I refuse to accept. Some of the biggest regrets we have occur when we say or do things while in a reactive mode. And I've got enough scar tissue to know what I'm talking about.

Well, it looks good on paper, doesn't it? Good advice is easy to write, and easy to read. I haven't said anything here that of all us haven't said to ourselves or others. But "The proof is in the pudding". And for me the secret of The Pudding is in the way we prompt ourselves to choose the appropriate behavior, and avoid the inappropriate one.

I have been a strong advocate for many years in using **Visual Prompts.** And, many students over the years have embraced my advocacy. Choose a behavior you want to engage in more or less, and prompt yourself to engage in it. It could be as simple as a sign over your office doorway stating 4 to 1; reminding you to look for 4 positives to every negative you find when you go on patrol.

It could be Listen over your phone, prompting you to do the obvious. And, when you find yourself becoming habit forming, reward yourself. Remember, good work should not go unnoticed.

Δ I've had about all I can stand of myself

Attributed to many

Approximately Right vs. Precisely Wrong

I recently assessed a leadership candidate that can best be described as taking a long time to reach a state of indecisiveness. I'm absolutely positive I will assess another one shortly, because they are literally everywhere. This was someone who had fairly good leadership instinct, but his drive for perfection buried him in such a morass of detail he wasn't able to see the forest, let alone individual trees. In fact all of us are a product of our experiences to varying degrees.

Many of us have been trained as "binary" thinkers --- Bank Auditors, Engineers, MIS (Management Information Services) folks have been trained and programmed to "find the right answers". When we bring these technical, management attributes to the leadership game, however, they often fall short because interpersonal relationships are based more on approximation than precision.

Δ It's better to be approximately right, than precisely wrong

Author unknown

Paralysis by Being Scared **less

You fill in the blank with what you are most comfortable with. You see, I'm practicing proper delegation. This is a phenomenon I associate many technocrats with, although we all come down with it occasionally. What this calls for is another *cosmic enema*. The symptoms are usually identifiable by what the experts call "lack of data".

The result is Paralysis. Webster defines paralysis as "a more or less complete crippling". In the workplace, however, this is a highly transmittable disease; crippling not only yourself, but others as well. We often see both visual and verbal proof of this malady in our Assessment Labs, where many managers and their respective participants are surprised with the diagnosis.

"He/She/I is/am very thorough in their projects and reports, and he/she/I excels at analyzing the data and anticipating risk. Well, Wunderkind, I got a newsflash for you. I don't give a rat's hinny about how good they are at their technical jobs, or how accurate they are with their analysis. Accept the fact that Management is different from Leadership. Deal with the fact that this is risky business.

Understand you will miss critical "moments of truth" because you are too wrapped up in detail. Accept the fact that administration and analytical skills are different than those used to stir souls and shape behaviors.

Interpersonally, you will probably never have enough data to quiet your internal Yama Yama (the little voice in you that tells you to be comfortable, or not). Interpersonal stuff is often non predictable until you're up to your eyeballs in it. Many of my students initially carve out a path based on their assumptions, and look for enough data to prove themselves right about you or me.

And their initial assumption was wrong to begin with. If the data doesn't fit, rather than look for other approaches, the majority of these folks get more entrenched in untenable positions. Even worse, they often miss what I call the "Window of Impact" that will make the biggest splash, and is based solely on timing. Get over the fear of not being right. Acknowledge to your subordinates up front that your initial assumptions may be wrong, but you'd like to explore them anyway.

Napkin Notes

- *Leadership is risky Business, If You Do It right.*
- *Lead in Excess, not in Moderation.*
- *Good Leaders are Good Actors.*
- *Leaders are Proactive, Not Reactive*
- *Binary thinkers are Poor Leaders. In Leadership, it's Often Better to be Approximately right than Precisely Wrong.*
- *Act Within the "Moments of Truth"; the Best Opportunities to Have Impact.*

Chapter 15: Followership

A great Chinese general many years ago stated "If you would lead, learn to follow". I believe this advice may be suspect in the heat of battle, when the troops are looking for their leaders and find them hunkered down in the rear echelon. However, it often is sound advice in the workplace environment. There is an art, science and responsibility to followership, just as in leadership. It is, however, often overlooked. I keep looking for a workshop to come out on it, and if you get there before I do, let me know.

There is a time to lead, and a time to allow others to lead. Good leaders understand the timing instinctively. One of the more visible roles that should contain these decisions is that of the Team Facilitator.

A Team Facilitator who is good at getting others in meeting deadlines may not be the best choice to lead a team through Creative Thinking. A Team Facilitator adept at problem solving may not do so well at implementation. And so on and so on. My own experience, seasoned with feedback from many others, is that being designated a Team Leader is more often than not similar to being elected to the Supreme Court.

It is a title for the life of the project. Although they may not verbalize it, I know what many of these so-called team leaders are saying: "It took me long enough to get this power. Why the hell should I give it to you?" Well, leading the team is one thing. Looking back to see if they're still following you is something altogether different. The two actions often do not coincide.

I'm A Good Leader

This statement has variations of truth, depending on who's saying it, and who's disputing it. I invariably ask for a second, third and twentieth opinion. The best views of leadership often come from those who follow; not those who lead. Feedback is the Breakfast of Leaders.

Those who avoid asking subordinates how they are doing, or what they could do better, in my opinion disgrace the title of Leader. There is certainly risk (which I've addressed earlier) in suffering the "slings and arrows" of outrageous subordinates. However, there is tremendous value and payoff in the saying that "what doesn't kill you will make you stronger". Leadership is a growth process.

Vitamins come from the results, but growth comes from the nutrients supplied by others. Morale Surveys should be conducted yearly, as should 360° feedback sessions for all those in a leadership capacity. Performance Appraisal Systems should include feedback from key subordinates, internal and external clients, etc. Leaders should be held accountable not only for the results, but for acting on those results.

Such accountability validates the input and associated risk in providing it by subordinates. As I often heard my Grandpa Black say while I lived with him on his Canadian farm:

> *Δ It's better to have*
> *10% of something,*
> *than 100% of nothing.*

Grandpa Black

Wish My Boss Had Been in this Workshop

I literally wish I had a dollar for every time I heard participants say this when leaving one of my workshops. First of all, most of the time I wish they had been there also, so I could chew them out directly. However, subordinates guilty of this statement also put themselves in my direct line of fire.

The outside consultant who shows up either before the battle begins, or after the smoke clears --- creates a safe haven for those who have a need to vent. But why aren't these people venting to their boss? Everyone is a subordinate to someone. I even find myself subordinate to my twelve year old granddaughter Peyton, which is something way beyond my ability to fathom or comprehend.

And yes, I will even admit that as her subordinate I often find myself ill at ease with giving her feedback. I understand the dynamics and risk of pushing "up the ladder". But Ignorance is no excuse for understanding The Law of Feedback.

The point is, bosses who continually "step in it" often have not had the benefit of feedback from their subordinates in order to adjust their course. I will acknowledge that, despite the feedback, some won't adjust and may even turn a "darker shade of Pale". However, many will, if we can just summon up the intestinal fortitude to approach them in a positive and non threatening way.

A Manufacturing Director I once worked for in Deering Milliken told me: "You must understand that you're on a train. Assume the train is presently heading North. You only have three (3) choices. If you've never been North, and you'd like to go, figure out how to help the train get there. If you don't want to go North, then you got to figure out how to turn the train around, or get the hell off the train!"

If you don't like what's going on, I submit to you the same three choices I had. And if you ever attend one of my workshops, don't you dare tell me you "wish your boss had been there". Been there; done that. Grandpa Black had this one covered as well, although he was more graphic about it than I can be:

Δ *If You're Not the Lead Dog, Your View is always gonna be pretty much the same.*

Attributed to many

The Drama Triangle

As introduced by Stephen Karpman --- I like his analogies and have been using the concept for years. The Triangle certainly holds true in the business setting, although it is probably used more in the Mental Health arena. (**SEE Figure Below**).

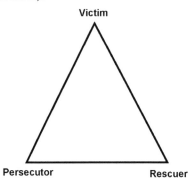

"Followership" is not the absence of delegation or accountability. Followership is a reasoned and calculated response to the situation at hand, incorporating both task and interpersonal development requirements. The premise is in and of itself fairly simple to follow.

It is much more difficult to avoid. Basically the Triangle tells us that when we (Rescuer) attempt to rescue someone(Victim) by taking their responsibility over or away from them, we will end up being "persecuted" by the very people (Victim turned Persecutor) we are attempting to rescue.

If a subordinate's report is late, and you tell him/her that you'll just go head and get it done for them, watch your back! You'll never do the report as well as they would have if they still had the responsibility for getting it done.

On a personal level, I tried to "rescue" my mom after my dad died. In my opinion at the time, she could have been the poster child for co-dependency. She didn't drive; she lived far away me in Florida and she didn't have many friends that I knew of. What a big dumb ass mistake I made!

There was a whole different side of my mom no one knew existed. When I basically coerced her to move in with my family and me, we were soon informed by my mother through several different verbal and visual channels that we were not doing as good a job running things as she could, if she still had the responsibility for herself. God bless her, she was still teaching me right up until the last.

Solving subordinate's problems for them is not only a bad answer; it's setting up bad precedence. The problem with being a hero is that there is a helluva lot more work to do than a hero can possibly handle. Be a leader; be a follower; but do not abdicate peoples' responsibility for doing their own job.

Δ *When I Say No; I Shouldn't Feel Guilty*

Dr. Manual Smith

Napkin Notes

- *Team Roles Should be Matched to Team Member Skills*
- *Good Leaders are Content to Allow Others to Lead*
- *Feedback is the Breakfast of Leaders*
- *Vitamins Come from Within. Nutrients to Grow Come from Others.*
- *Don't "Rescue" People by Taking Their Responsibility Away from Them.*
- *How Do Your Subordinates View You as a Leader?*
- *Bosses Often need to be Trained by Their Subordinates*

Chapter 16: You Are SOL

Surely you've heard the phrase "You're SOL". If you're thinking the same thing I am, we will agree SOL is an unenviable position managers often find themselves in. However, in order not to offend the delicate constitutions of those of you not conversant in common workplace language, let's just call SOL "Sorta Outa Luck".

Let me set this one up for you. In the past two years I've worked with several large organizations in getting ready to "ramp up" for increased productivity. Correctly, at the time management saw the need to set up a separate training function to handle large, untrained additions to the workforce.

Strategically they saw the need to dedicate some of their best people to training their new hires, and initially began to organize around this premise. Unfortunately, management lacked the tactical discipline to follow through. When the pressure was to produce, and the pressure to produce became constant, the temptation to take experienced, trained trainers away from training and return them to production was often too great. The results were predictable.

As a Training Manager who reported directly to a GM, some of my most memorable fights were with production managers who strategically couldn't find their own butt with the help of a high-end GPS . If they're lucky, they can get production out of unskilled labor while reducing waste and off quality.

There is always pressure to keep productivity up on a daily basis. However, what is achieved by putting unskilled labor on highly skilled work? While you may increase productivity, you are also increasing the production of waste, recall, and in manufacturing, variables such as lost time accidents.

Allow employees time to be trained correctly, and you may take hits in productivity short term, but are always much better off from a quality standpoint long term. Do I really need to make the point that it is better to keep a few customers happy, as opposed to "p'off" a large number of them?

Because of my highly developed skills of persuasion, I actually believed I had these organizations convinced of the strategic importance of an independent training program that could advocate and monitor best training methods. But as soon as I turned my back, management in both organizations caved in to the "urgency of the task".

Highly skilled full time trainers were relegated back to running full time jobs, only occasionally participating in the "Sit by Nellie" on job training described earlier in the book. Recalls and warranty work is presently going through the ceiling. Putting full time Trainers under the direction of tactically oriented production managers and supervisors is akin to putting chickens in a fox den. Try asking a hungry fox to allow the chickens to continue laying eggs. You can't have it both ways!

Synchronous Flow and Theory of Constraints

Synchronous Flow and Theory of Constraints teach us that if we don't control our bottlenecks through the establishment of "Choke Points", we leave our outcomes to chance. Deming and Goldratt were not stupid people, and they didn't trust process outcomes to luck.

The same holds true to employee development. It is in and of itself a process that must be strategically controlled. Luck will only work if you're a good swimmer. Learn control, and don't over commit to producing what your skill level can't accommodate.

> *Δ Luck may provide breakfast,*
> *but don't count on it to show*
> *up for dinner.*

Tom Fehlman

Empowerment vs. Ownership

Empowerment is one of those really cool "consulting terms" we consultants dream up so we can charge you more for the next round of books and workshops. I'm looking for someone to explain to me how we can hire someone for a job, come back to them in the future and have to empower them to actually do the job we've hired them for. Ownership is not a new concept.

It goes back to the cave days, when entrepreneurial spear makers made spears for themselves and others. If the spear didn't work, assuming the spear makers were still alive after their feedback with a highly agitated spear thrower, they owned the responsibility of the faulty spear. Ownership involves taking responsibility, applying initiative and accepting risk. Ownership is not <u>management abdication.</u> It involves employee development, training, delegation, trust and risking-taking on the part of the leader.

> *Δ Leaders know when to fire,*
> *and when to fall back..*
>
> Tom Fehlman

Cave to the Cabin to the Complex

Thousands of years ago, if you wanted a spear, you made it yourself. Ingenuity was the Mother of Survival. As time wore on, some found they had a "knack" for making flint knives; others for making spears, and others for sticking their hands in mud and making pictures on walls.

Now, if I wanted a spear, I found a really good Spearmaker, went to his cave and exchanged my handprints on his wall for one of his well-made spears. If his spear failed me, and if I was physically able to register a complaint after the spear broke, he and I would have a direct dialogue about his faulty spear. This was customer-supplier relationship in its purest form.

However, when the Spearmaker wanted to move to a better neighborhood, in a more upscale cave, he had to begin to market, and direct customer-supplier relationships began to expand and change beyond personal control.

The more complex our organizations become, the more diluted ownership becomes. It has become increasingly convenient to be able to hide responsibility and authority behind teams, processes and programs. When I see an organization with more than two levels of responsibility, I see tremendous gaps between how much authority the senior level believes the lower level has, and the actual authority the lowest level believes they have. If you doubt me, develop a list of simple job duties you expect from your subordinates, and more importantly, for subordinates under them.

Ask your folks how much Responsibility and Authority they believe they have to carry these duties out. Compare your list to theirs, take some strong drugs and go right to bed. There will be up to 75% difference between how you see it, and how they actually feel it. Surprisingly, this is a topic that seldom comes up, and consequently is seldom addressed. Supervisors are waiting for some type of empowerment. Senior management is P.Oed because their supervision is not demonstrating any initiative or risk taking. HELLO?

> *Δ Reality is just a crutch*
> *for those people who can't*
> *handle drugs.*
>
> Lily Tomlin

Take Pictures of the Japanese

Maybe it's time we start taking pictures of them. I remember back in the day when workplaces were replete with Japanese visitors and "tourists" taking pictures of everything that moved. Some of us found this behavior amusing and at times even fascinating. Several decades ago I was sent to a Japanese textile mill to observe how Quality Circles worked in that environment.

When I entered the plant I noticed ribbons hanging off of ceilings, railings and walls. Asking my guide the reason for the ribbons, he replied that their floor sweepers (incidentally, an entry level job) had figured out on their own that dust and lint were major factors in the quality weaving of their cloth.

Evidently, on their own initiative they decided that if they could track airflow within the plant, they would know where to sweep more often. This action had absolutely nothing to do with "Empowerment", and it happened to me over thirty years ago. No one told these floor sweepers to engage in this activity. There in fact was a "delightful absence" of management involvement.

When I walk into a production area, I can tell how much ownership is around by who and how many people come up to me and remind me that safety glasses are required in that area. If managers have to hunt me down they're usually between the latest fads in Empowerment training. When employees immediately come up to me and remind me of the glasses, I can say with absolute certainty that at least when it comes to safety, that environment is full of Ownership.

> *Δ Ownership occurs in the*
> *delightful absence of*
> *management*
>
> Tom Fehlman

Leadership Through Partnership

Not long ago I finished an assignment which basically involved getting management and labor to "play nice" with each other. The initial struggle was to get Senior Leadership from both Management and Labor to trust their own team, let alone trust anybody else. It was a classic story of "Us vs. Them", which is misleading because when you threw in supervisors and shop stewards into the mix, it was more like "Us vs. Them vs. Those Guys".

Nobody trusted anybody anywhere. There was a lot of 'scar tissue" everywhere. When I drilled down into the supervisor and shop steward group, it became very apparent that they wanted the environment to change as much as anyone. However, they were not considered part of the leadership team.

Their historic roles were to fight for either task or relationships, respectively. Supervisors and Stewards are now working together to solve common workplace problems. They are not allowed to push problems "up" until they have tried collectively to solve the problem.

The first step was get to Senior Leadership to sign a mutual pact outlining agreed upon value drivers and non negotiable workplace requirements. This initiative came from the General Manager, who finally realized his micro management was greatly hindering needed flexibility in the workplace.

Incidentally, I give him great credit for his personal re-assessment of his leadership qualities. When I got to the supervisor and steward level, the initial task was to get them to realize how much their "baggage" about everything that had ever been done to them was getting in the way of progress.

The next challenge was to expose to them how much power they had over the work environment, and how much both groups actually had in common such as safety, job security and productivity. At one time I had to get both groups upset with me just to prove that point. Senior Management finally "Empowered" them to take action.

What no one (except myself) anticipated is that once they were empowered, supervisors and stewards became proactive in their **ownership**. They decided to present their Partnership Agreements to the entire workforce, and when the plant manager suggested they attach the Partnership Meeting to one of his workplace meetings, the Leadership Team of Supervisors and Shop Stewards told him they didn't want him involved in this meeting.

The Leadership Team realized they knew where the productivity and employee problems were, better than management did. Once management trusted them to deal with these problems without always getting permission, Ownership took place.

Empowerment is only a step to Ownership. If you introduce the idea of Empowerment to your employees, without the ultimate goal of Ownership, you will end up in a worse position than when you started the process. Once people taste some input and control over their own environment, they will not give it up easily.

You can trust 80% of your people to handle ownership responsively and effectively. That's all you need, but at the risk of repeating myself, also be prepared to deal directly with your 20% "Seeds of Satan".

Napkin Notes

- *Don't Confuse Ownership with Empowerment*
- *Push Problems Down' Not Up*
- *Find out What Other Organizations Are Doing. Benchmark.*
- *Don't Mistrust Many because You Can't Trust a Few.*
- *If You Promise Empowerment, be Prepared to Handle Ownership.*
- *Don't Commit to What You Can't Produce*
- *Take the Time to Train*
- *Re-consider Having Trainers Reporting to Operations*
- *Employee Training Should be a Controlled Process*

Chapter 17: Here's Your Halo

This chapter is dedicated to all those managers whose leadership "halos" may fit just a little too tight. Few of us are actually as good as we would like to believe. Consider these questions a "wakeup" call for those of us who have lulled ourselves into a false sense of being pretty damn good.

Answer these questions honestly. Look at the types and quality of data you actually have available that lead you to answer the way you do. Are your answers based on actual data, or assumptions, or hope? From a leadership perspective, these questions and their resultant answers dictate the type of "leaderful" organization you are helping to create.

Here's Your Halo

Do they really believe it?

We Are Customer Driven **Here's Your Halo**
Do Customers or "Silos" drive your organization?

Risk Taking is Rewarded **Here's Your Halo**
How and Why?

We Have an Open Door Policy **Here's Your Halo**
How many people use it?

My People Trust Me **Here's Your Halo**
How many of them do you trust?

Performance Appraisals Really Count **Here's Your Halo**
Is management held accountable for follow through?

We Select Leaders Carefully **Here's Your Halo**
Are you using the right skill sets?

People Are Held Accountable **Here's Your Halo**
Do you have an organization in which not everyone can work?

Don't Surround Me by "Yes Men" **Here's Your Halo**
Do your people really feel free to dissent?

We Believe in Training **Here's Your Halo**
In tough times, what gets cut out of your budget first?

Our People's Morale is High **Here's Your Halo**
Where's your data?

I Care About My People **Here's Your Halo**
Do your people go through walls for you, or do you push them through walls?

Supervisors Are Part of the Management Team   **Here's Your Halo**
Have they actually told you they are?

We Don't Need a Union Here   **Here's your Halo**
How do you know what your workforce is thinking?

Our Processes Are Standardized   **Here's Your Halo**
Are your Training and Re-training processes standardized?

Look at Our Beautiful Mission Statement   **Here's Your Halo**
Do people sweeping your floors understand it?

We Are Committed to this Program   **Here's Your Halo**
Do your people feel "This too shall pass"?

We Are Team Oriented   **Here's Your Halo**
Why?

We Are Process Driven   **Here's Your Halo**
Are rewards and recognition based on silos or processes?

Family is Important   **Here's Your Halo**
When did you last communicate with employees' families?

Our People Are Happy   **Here's Your Halo**
When was your last morale survey?

He/She is well qualified   **Here's Your Halo**
Are you using the right measurements?

I Listen to My People   **Here's Your Halo**
How often are they allowed to talk?

We Meet Our Deadlines   **Here's Your Halo**
How many of your people are you burning up?

We Do Things Right   **Here's Your Halo**
Would your customers still be willing to pay for it, if they
knew what you were doing?

Last Word: Leaderful Organizations

I love the term "Leaderful Organizations". I first hear it on a video "Leadership: the New Science" by Dr. Margaret Wheatley years ago. She stated she had heard the phrase expressed by someone else, so who knows where it came from. The important thing is that somebody said something for once in the consulting business that actually bears repeating.

I want to end this reading on an optimistic note. When I find myself optimistic about the future of leadership in our organizations, I can sometimes attribute it to a bout of being over-served with incurable romantics the day before. Or I'm tempted to actually believe what politicians tell me during the current political campaign.

Such is not the case at the time of this writing. After having just finished a leadership assessment of 10 potential candidates, I actually found several "eager beavers" who are potentially salvageable. Having assessed over 7,000 leadership candidates over the past twenty years, potential leaders continue to pop up, albeit it at an alarmingly slow rate. The problem is really not how many candidates I find. The issue centers around what we do with them when we find them.

I was told recently by a client they just realized that when they fill young peoples' heads up with all the potential for advancement they possess, there damn well better be something in the near future in the way of advancement that happens to them. That is a serious problem in terms of recruiting and retention, not to mention issues of morale and associated maladies.

My premise is that this is a systemic problem brought about basically by a lack of clear career paths with benchmarks, expected learning curves and identified apprenticeships in balanced task/relationship positions. If you can't measure it, you can't manage it.

I've always believed that organizations should be set up around relationships based upon internal customer and supplier requirements, and not driven by boss-subordinate relationships. I believe that successful leaders earn power and influence through their actions, and not through their titles or entitlements. I also believe that organizations should reward accomplishments based on strategic leadership as well as the accomplishment of tactical tasks.

Leaderful is such a beautiful concept, because it involves all the things we as leaders should strive to achieve. It is possible to create a workplace where people find both challenge and security. Most Employees who want to be held accountable, can be provided meaningful rewards for meeting their accountability.

We can uncover mutual values and belief systems that will create organizations in which not everyone can work. It is even possible to provide a work environment in which people actually look forward to working in. It is more than an art, but less than a science. We are surrounded by inexpensive, easily-picked "Low Hanging Fruit" that have been ignored by managers for years. All we have to do is listen and watch for the continuous opportunities our employees provide us to become leaders.

*Δ **We should create organizations in which not everyone belongs.***

Tom Fehlman